Laurier: A Study in Canadian Politics

J. W. Dafoe

LAURIER: A STUDY IN CANADIAN POLITICS

By J. W. DAFOE

1922

DEDICATION:
TO E. H. MACKLIN IN
ACKNOWLEDGEMENT OF A CONSTANT FRIENDSHIP.

PREFACE

The four articles which make up this volume were originally published in successive issues of the Monthly Book Review of the Manitoba Free Press and are herewith assembled in book form in response to what appears to be a somewhat general request that they be made available in a more permanent form.

J. W. D.
October 13 1922.

CONTENTS

PART ONE. LAURIER: A STUDY IN CANADIAN POLITICS

THE CLIMB TO POWER.

THE life story of Laurier by Oscar D. Skelton is the official biography of Sir Wilfrid Laurier. Official biographies of public men have their uses; they supply material for the definitive biography which in the case of a great man is not likely to be written by one who knew him in the flesh. An English public man, who was also a novelist and poet, wrote:

"Ne'er of the living can the living judge,
Too blind the affection or too fresh the grudge."

The limitation is equally true in the case of one like Sir Wilfrid Laurier who, though dead, will be a factor of moment in our politics for at least another generation. Professor Skelton's book is interesting and valuable, but not conclusive. The first volume is a political history of Canada from the sixties until 1896, with Laurier in the setting at first inconspicuously but growing to greatness and leadership. For the fifteen years of premiership the biographer is concerned lest Sir Wilfrid should not get the fullest credit for whatever was achieved; while in dealing with the period after 1911, constituting the anti-climax of Laurier's career, Mr. Skelton is avowedly the alert and eager partisan, bound to find his hero right and all those who disagreed with him wrong. Sir Wilfrid Laurier is described in the preface as "the finest and simplest gentleman, the noblest and most unselfish man it has ever been my good fortune to know; " and the work is faithfully devoted to the elucidation of this theme. Men may fail to be heroes to their valets but they are more successful with their biographers. The final appraisement of Sir Wilfrid, to be written perhaps fifty years hence by some tolerant and impartial historian, will probably not be an echo of Prof. Skelton's judgment. It will perhaps put Sir Wilfrid higher than Prof. Skelton does and yet not quite so high; an abler man but one not quite so preternaturally good; a man who had affinities with Macchiavelli as well as with Sir Galahad.

The Laurier of the first volume is an appealing, engaging and most attractive personality. There was about his earlier career something romantic and compelling. In almost one rush he passed from the comparative obscurity of a new member in 1874 to the leadership of the French Liberals in 1877; and then he suffered a decline which seemed to mark him as one of those political shooting stars which blaze in the firmament for a season and then go black; like Felix Geoffrion who, though saluted by Laurier in 1874 as the coming leader, never made any impress upon his times. A political accident, fortunate for him, opened the gates again to a career; and he set his foot upon a road which took him very far.

The writer made acquaintance with Laurier in the Dominion session of 1884. He was then in his forty-third year; but in the judgment of many his career was over. His interest in politics was, apparently, of the slightest. He was deskmate to Blake, who carried on a tremendous campaign that session against the government's C. P. R. proposals. Laurier's political activities consisted chiefly of being an acting secretary of sorts to the Liberal leader. He kept his references in order; handed him Hansards and blue-books in turn; summoned the pages to clear away the impedimenta and to keep the glass of water replenished—little services which it was clear he was glad to do for one who engaged his ardent affection and admiration. There were memories in the house of Laurier's eloquence; but memories only. During this session he was almost silent. The tall, courtly figure was a familiar sight in the chamber and in the library—particularly in the library, where he could be found every day ensconced in some congenial alcove; but the golden voice was silent. It was known that his friends were concerned about his health.

LAURIER AND THE RIEL AGITATION

The "accident" which restored Laurier to public life and opened up for him an extraordinary career was the Riel rebellion of 1885. In the session of 1885, the rebellion being then in progress, he was heard from to some purpose on the subject of the ill treatment of the Saskatchewan half-breeds by the Dominion government. The execution of Riel in the following November changed the whole course of Canadian politics. It pulled the foundations from under the Conservative party by destroying the position of supremacy which it had held for a generation in the most Conservative of provinces and condemned it to a slow decline to the ruin of to-day; and it profoundly affected the Liberal party, giving it a new orientation and producing the leader who was to make it the dominating force in Canadian politics. These things were not realized at the time, but they are clear enough in retrospect. Party policy, party discipline, party philosophy are all determined by the way the constituent elements of the party combine; and the shifting from the Conservative to the Liberal party of the political weight of Quebec, not as the result of any profound change of conviction but under the influence of a powerful racial emotion, was bound to register itself in time in the party outlook and morale. The current of the older tradition ran strong for some time, but within the space of about twenty years the party was pretty thoroughly transformed. The Liberal party of to-day with its complete dependence upon the solid support it gets in Quebec is the ultimate result of the forces which came into play as the result of the hanging of Riel.

After the lapse of so many years there is no need for lack of candor in discussing the events of 1885. To put it plainly Riel's fate turned almost entirely upon political considerations. Which was the less dangerous course, —to reprieve him or let him hang? The issue was canvassed back and forth by the distracted ministry up to the day before that fixed for the execution when a decision was reached to let the law take its course. The feeling in Quebec in support of the commutation was so intense and overwhelming that it was accepted as a matter of course that Riel would be reprieved; and the news of the contrary decision was to them, as Professor Skelton says, "unbelievable. " The actual announcement of the hanging was a match to a powder magazine. That night there were mobs on the streets of Montreal and Sir John Macdonald was burned in effigy in Dominion square. On the following Sunday forty thousand people swarmed around the hustings on Champ de Mars and heard the government denounced in every conceivable term of verbal violence by speakers of every tinge of political belief. This outpouring of a common indignation with its obliteration of all the usual lines of demarcation was the result of the "wounding of the national self-esteem" by the flouting of the demand for leniency, as it was put by La Minerve. Mercier put it still more strongly when he declared that "the murder of Riel was a declaration of war upon French Canadian influence in Confederation. " A binding cement for this union of elements ordinarily at war was sought for in the creation of the "parti national" which a year later captured the provincial Conservative citadel at Quebec and turned it over to Honore Mercier. This violent racial movement raged unchecked in the provincial arena, but in the federal field it was held in leash by Laurier. That he saw the possibilities of the situation is not to be doubted. He took part in the demonstration on Champ de Mars and in his speech 'made a declaration—"Had I been born on the banks of the Saskatchewan I myself would have shouldered a musket"—

which riveted nation-wide attention upon him. Laurier followed this by his impassioned apology for the halfbreeds and their leader in the House of Commons, of which deliverance Thomas White, of the assailed ministry, justly said: "It was the finest parliamentary speech ever pronounced in the parliament of Canada since Confederation. " In the debate on the execution of Riel all the orators of parliament took part. It was the occasion for one of Blake's greatest efforts. Sir John Thompson, in his reply to Blake, revealed himself to parliament and the country as one worthy of crossing swords with the great Liberal tribune. But they and all the other "big guns" of the Commons were thrown into complete eclipse by Laurier's performance. It is easy to recall after the lapse of thirty-six years the extraordinary impression which that speech made upon the great audience which heard it—a crowded House of Commons and the public galleries packed to the roof.

In the early winter of 1886-7 Laurier went boldly into Ontario where, addressing great audiences in Toronto, London and other points, he defended his position and preferred his indictment against the government. This was Laurier's first introduction to Ontario, under circumstances which, while actually threatening, were in reality auspicious. It was at once an exhibition of moral and physical courage and a manifestation of Laurier's remarkable qualities as a public speaker. Within a few months Laurier passed from the comparative obscurity to which he had condemned himself by his apparent indifference to politics to a position in public life where he divided public attention and interest with Edward Blake and Sir John Macdonald. When a few months later Blake, in a rare fit of the sulks, retired to his tent, refusing to play any longer with people who did not appreciate his abilities, Laurier succeeded to the leadership— apparently upon the nomination of Blake, actually at the imperious call of those inescapable forces and interests which men call Destiny.

LEADERSHIP AND THE ROAD TO IT.

Laurier, then in his 46th year, became leader of the Liberal party in June, 1887. It was supposedly a tentative experimental choice; but the leadership thus begun ended only with his death in February, 1919, nearly thirty-two years later. Laurier was a French Canadian of the ninth generation. His first Canadian ancestor, Augustin Hebert, was one of the little band of soldier colonists who, under the leadership of Maisonneuve founded Montreal in 1641. Hebert's granddaughter married a soldier of the regiment Carignan-Salieres,

Francois Cotineau dit Champlaurier. The Heberts were from Normandy, Cotineau from Savoy. From this merging of northern and southern French strains the Canadian family of Laurier resulted; this name was first assumed by the grandson of the soldier ancestor. The record of the first thirty years of Wilfrid Laurier's life was indistinguishable from that of scores of other French-Canadian professional men. Born in the country (St. Lin, Nov. 20, 1841) of parents in moderate circumstances; educated at one of the numerous little country colleges; a student at law in Montreal; a young and struggling lawyer, interested in politics and addicted upon occasion to political journalism. —French-Canadians by the hundreds have travelled that road. A fortunate combination of circumstances took him out of the struggle for a place at the Montreal bar and gave him a practice in the country combined with the editorship of a Liberal weekly, a position which made him at once a figure of some local prominence. Laurier's personal charm and obvious capacity for politics marked him at once for local leadership. At the age of 30 he was sent to the Quebec legislature as representative of the constituency of Drummond and Arthabaska; and three years later he went to Ottawa. The rapid retirement of the Rouge leaders, Dorion and Fournier to the bench and Letellier to the lieutenant-governorship of Quebec, opened the way for early promotion, and in 1877 he entered the cabinet of Alex. Mackenzie and assumed at the same time the leadership of the French Liberals. Defeated in Drummond-Arthabaska upon seeking re-election he was taken to its heart by Quebec East and continued to represent that constituency for an unbroken period of forty years. He went out of office with Mackenzie in 1878, and thereafter his career which had begun so promisingly dwindled almost to extinction until the events already noted called him back to the lists and opened for him the doors of opportunity.

When Wilfrid Laurier went to Montreal in 1861 he began the study of law in the office of Rodolphe Laflamme, a leading figure in the Rouge political group; and he joined L'Institut Canadien already far advanced in the struggle with the church which was later to result in open warfare. Those two acts revealed his political affiliations and fixed the environment in which he was to move during the plastic twenties. Ten years had passed since a group of ardent young men, infected with the principles and enthusiasm of 1848, of which Papineau returning from exile in Paris was the apostle, had stormed the constituencies of Lower Canada and had appeared in the parliament of Canada as a radical, free-thinking, ultra-Democratic party, bearing proudly the badge of "Rouge"; and the passage of time was beginning to temper their views with a tinge of sobriety. The church, however, had them all in her black books and Bishop Bourget, that incomparable zealot and bigot, was determined to destroy them politically and spiritually, to whip them into submission. The struggle raged chiefly in the sixties about L'Institut Canadien, frowned upon by the church because it had books in its library which were banned by the Index and because it afforded a free forum for discussion. When Confederation cut the legislative connection between Upper and Lower Canada the church felt itself free to proceed to extremes in the Catholic province of Quebec and embarked upon that campaign of political proscription which ultimately reached a point where even the Rome of Pius IX. felt it necessary to intervene.

In this great battle for political and intellectual freedom the young Laurier played his part manfully. He boldly joined L'Institut Canadien, though it lay under the shadow of Bishop Bourget's minatory pastoral; and became an active member and officer. He was one of a committee which tried unavailingly to effect an understanding with Bishop Bourget. When he left Montreal in 1866 he was first vice-president of the Institute. His native caution and prudence and his natural bent towards moderation and accommodation enabled him to play a great and growing, though non-spectacular, part in the struggle against the church's pretensions. As his authority grew in the party he discouraged the excesses in theory and speech which invited the Episcopal thunders; even in his earliest days his radicalism was of a decidedly Whiggish type and his political color was several shades milder than the fiery red of Papineau, Dorion and Laflamme. Under his guidance the Rouge party was to be transformed in outlook, mentality and convictions into something very different indeed; but this was still far in the future. But towards the church's pretensions to control the political convictions of its adherents he presented an unyielding front. On the eve of his assumption of the leadership of the French Liberals he discussed at Quebec, June 1877, the question of the political relations between church and state and the rights of the individual in one of his most notable addresses. In this he vindicated, with eloquence and courage, the right of the individual to be both Catholic and Liberal, and challenged the policy of clerical intimidation which had made the leaders of the church nothing but the tools and chore-boys of Hector Langevin, the Tory leader in the province. It may rightly be assumed that it was something more than a coincidence that not long after the delivery of this speech, Rome put a bit in the mouth of the champing Quebec ecclesiastics. This remained Laurier's most solid achievement up to the time when he was called to the leadership of the Dominion Liberal party.

DOUBTS AND HESITATIONS

Laurier's accession to leadership caused doubt and heart-burnings among the leaders of Ontario Liberalism. Still under the influence of the Geo. Brown tradition of suspicion of Quebec they felt uneasy at the transfer of the sceptre to Laurier, French by inheritance, Catholic in religion, with a political experience derived from dealing with the feelings, ambitions and prejudices of a province which was to them an unknown world. Part of the doubt arose from misconception of the qualities of Laurier. As a hard-bitten, time-worn party fighter, with an experience going back to pre-confederation days, said to the writer: "Laurier will never make a leader; he has not enough of the devil in him. " This meant, in the brisk terminology of to-day, that he could not deliver the rough stuff. This doubter and his fellows had yet to learn that the flashing rapier in the hands of the swordsman makes a completer and far less messy job than the bludgeon; and that there is in politics room for the delicate art of jiu-jitsu. Further, the Ontario mind was under the sway of that singular misconception, so common to Britishers, that a Frenchman by temperament is gay, romantic, inconsequent, with few reserves of will and perseverance. Whereas the good French mind is about the coolest, clearest, least emotional instrument of the kind that there is. The courtesy, grace, charm, literary and artistic ability that go with it are merely accessories; they are the feathers on the arrow that help it in its flight from the twanging bow-cord to the bull's-eye. Laurier's mind was typically French with something also Italianate about it, an inheritance perhaps from the long-dead Savoyard ancestor who brought the name to this continent. Later when Laurier had proved his quality and held firmly in his hands the reins of power, the fatuous Ontario Liberal explained him as that phenomenon, a man of pure French ancestry who was spiritually an Englishman—this conclusion being drawn from the fact that upon occasion the names of Charles James Fox and Gladstone came trippingly from his tongue. The new relationship between the Liberals and Laurier was entered upon with obvious hesitation on the part of many of the former and by apparent diffidence by the latter. It may be that the conditional acceptance and the proffered resignation at call were tactical movements really intended by Laurier to buttress his position as leader, as most assuredly his frequent suggestions of a readiness or intention to retire during the last few years of his leadership were. But, whatever the uncertainties of the moment, they soon passed. Laurier at once showed capacities which the Liberals had never before known in a leader. The long story of Liberal sterility and ineffectiveness from the middle of the last century to almost its close is the story of the political incapacity of its successive leaders, a demonstration of the unfitness of men with the emotional equipment of the pamphleteer, crusader and agitator for the difficult business of party management. The party sensed almost immediately the difference in the quality of the new leadership; and liked it. Laurier's powers of personal charm completed the "consolidation of his position, " and by the early nineties the Presbyterian Grits of Ontario were swearing by him. When Blake, after two or three years of nursing his wounds in retirement, began to think it was time to resume the business of leading the Liberals, he found everywhere invisible barriers blocking his return. Laurier was, he found, a different proposition from Mackenzie; and there was nothing for it but to return to his tent and take farewell of his constituents in that tale of lamentations, the West Durham letter. The new regime, the new leadership, did not bring results at once. The party experienced a succession of unexpected and unforeseen misfortunes that almost made Laurier superstitious. "Tell me, " he wrote to his friend Henri Beaugrand, in August, 1891, "whether there is not some fatality pursuing our party. " In the election of 1891 not even the theatricality of Sir John Macdonald's last appeal nor the untrue claim by the government that it was about, itself, to secure a reciprocal trade arrangement with Washington, could have robbed the Liberals of a triumph which seemed certain; it was the opportune revelation, through the stealing of proofs from a printing office, that Edward Farrer, one of the Globe editors, favored political union with the United States, that gave victory into the hands of the Conservatives. But their relatively narrow majority would not have kept them in office a year in view of the death of Sir John A. Macdonald in June, 1891, and the stunning blows given the government by the "scandal session" of 1891, had it not been for two disasters which overtook the Liberals: The publication of Blake's letter and the revelation of the rascalities of the Mercier regime. Perhaps of the two blows, that delivered by Blake was the more disastrous. The letter was the message of an oracle. It required an interpretation which the oracle refused to supply; and in its absence the people regarded it as implying a belief by Blake that annexation was the logical sequel to the Liberal policy of unrestricted reciprocity. The result was seen in the by-election campaign of 1892 when the Liberals lost seat after seat in Ontario, and the government majority mounted to figures which suggested that the party, despite the loss of Sir John, was as strong as ever. The Tories were in the seventh heaven of delight. With the Liberals broken, humiliated and discouraged, and a young and vigorous pilot, in the person of Sir John Thompson, at the helm, they saw a long and happy voyage before them. Never were appearances more illusory, for the cloud was already in the sky from which were to come storm, tempest and ruinous   over-throw.

THE TACTICS OF VICTORY

The story of the Manitoba school question and the political struggle which centred around it, as told by Prof. Skelton, is bald and colorless; it gives little sense of the atmosphere of one of the most electrical periods in our history. The sequelae of the Riel agitation, with its stirring up of race feeling, included the Jesuit Estates controversy in parliament, the Equal Rights movement in Ontario, the attack upon the use of the French language in the legislature of the Northwest Territories and the establishment of a system of National schools in Manitoba through the repeal of the existing school law, which had been modelled upon the Quebec law and was intended to perpetuate the double-barrelled system in vogue in that province. The issue created by the Manitoba legislation projected itself at once into the federal field to the evident consternation of the Dominion government. It parried the demand for disallowance of the provincial statute by an engagement to defray the cost of litigation challenging the validity of the law. When the Privy Council, reversing the judgment of the Supreme Court, found that the law was valid because it did not prejudicially affect rights held prior to or at the time of union, the government was faced with a demand that it intervene by virtue of the provisions in the British North America act, which gave the Dominion parliament the power to enact remedial educational legislation overriding provincial enactments in certain circumstances. Again it took refuge in the courts. The Supreme Court of Canada held that under the circumstances the power to intervene did not exist; and the government breathed easier. Again the Privy Council reversed the judgment of the Supreme Court and held that because the Manitoba law prejudicially affected educational privileges enjoyed by the minority after union there was a right of intervention. The last defence of the Dominion government against being forced to make a decision was broken down; in the language of to-day, it was up against it. And the man who might have saved the party by inducing the bishops of the Catholic church to moderate their demands was gone, for Sir John Thompson died in Windsor Castle in December, 1894, one month before the Privy Council handed down its fateful decision. Sir John was a faithful son of the church, with an immense influence with the clerical authorities; he was succeeded in the premiership by Sir Mackenzie Bowell, ex-grand master of the Orange Order. The bishops moved on Ottawa and demanded action.

There ensued a duel in tactics between the two parties, intensely interesting in character and in its results surprising, at least for some people. The parties to the struggle which now proceeded to convulse Canada were the government of Manitoba, the author of the law in question, the Roman Catholic hierarchy in their capacity of guardians and champions of the Manitoba minority, and the two Dominion political parties. The bishops were in deadly earnest in attack; so was the Manitoba government in defence; but with the others the interest was purely tactical. How best to set the sails to catch the veering winds and blustering gusts to win the race, the prize for which was the government of Canada? The Conservatives had the right of initiative—did it give them the advantage? They thought so; and so did most of the Liberal generals who were mostly in a blue funk during the year 1895 in anticipation of the hole into which the government was going to place them. But there was at least one Liberal tactician who knew better.

The Conservatives decided upon a line of action which seemed to them to have the maximum of advantage. They would go in for remedial legislation. In the English provinces they would say that they did this reluctantly as good, loyal, law-abiding citizens obeying the order of the Queen delivered through the Privy Council. From their experiences with the electors they had good reason to believe that this buncombe would go down. But in Quebec they would pose as the defenders of the oppressed, loyal co-operators with the bishops in rebuking, subduing and chaining the Manitoba tyrants. Obviously they would carry the province; if Laurier opposed their legislation they would sweep the province and he would be left without a shred of the particular support which was supposed to be his special contribution to a Liberal victory. The calculation looked good to the Conservatives; also to most of the Liberals. As one Liberal veteran put it in 1895: "If we vote against remedial legislation we shall be lost, hook, line and sinker. " But there was one Liberal who thought differently.

His name was J. Israel Tarte. Tarte was in office an impossibility; power went to his head like strong wine and destroyed him. But he was the man whose mind conceived, and whose will executed, the Napoleonic stroke of tactics which crumpled up the Conservative army in 1896 and put it in the hole which had been dug for the Liberals. On the day in March, 1895, when the Dominion government issued its truculent and imperious remedial order, Tarte said to the present writer: "The government is in the den of lions; if only Greenway will now shut the door. " At that early day he saw with a clearness of vision that was never afterwards clouded, the tactics that meant victory: "Make the party policy suit the campaign in the other provinces; leave Quebec to Laurier and me. " He foresaw that the issue in Quebec would not be made by the government nor by the bishops; it would be whether the French-Canadians, whose imagination and affections had already been captured by Laurier, would or would not vote to put their great man in the chair of the prime minister of Canada. All through the winter and spring of 1895 Tarte was sinking test wells in Quebec public opinion with one uniform result. The issue was Laurier. So the policy was formulated of marking time until the government was irretrievably committed to remedial legislation; then the Liberals as a solid body were to throw themselves against it. So Laurier and the Liberal party retired within the lines of Torres Vedras and bided their time.

But Tarte had no end of trouble in keeping the party to the path marked out. The fainthearts of the other provinces could not keep from their minds the haunting fear that the road they were marching along led to a morass. They wanted a go-as-you please policy by which each section of the party could make its own appeal to local feeling. Laurier was never more indecisive than in the war councils in which these questions of party policy were fought over. And with good reason. His sympathy and his judgment were with Tarte but he feared to declare himself too pronouncedly. The foundation stone of Tarte's policy was a belief in the overwhelming potency of Laurier's name in Quebec; Laurier was naturally somewhat reluctant to put his own stock so high. He had not yet come to believe implicitly in his star. Within forty-eight hours of the time when Laurier made his speech moving the six months' hoist to the Remedial bill, a group of Liberal sub-chiefs from the English provinces made a resolute attempt to vary the policy determined upon. Their bright idea was that Clarke Wallace, the seceding cabinet minister and Orange leader, should move the six months' hoist; this would enable the Liberals to divide, some voting for it and some against it. But the bold idea won. With Laurier's speech of March 3, 1896, the death-blow was given to the Conservative administration and the door to office and power opened to the Liberals.

The campaign absolutely vindicated the tactical foresight of Tarte. A good deal might be said about that campaign if space were available. But one or two features of it may be noted. In the English provinces great play was made with Father Lacombe's minatory letter to Laurier, sent while the issue was trembling in the balance in parliament: "If the government .. is beaten .. I inform you with regret that the episcopacy, like one man, united with the clergy, will rise to support those who may have fallen in defending us. " In his Reminiscences, Sir John Willison speculates as to how this letter, so detrimental to the government in Ontario, got itself published. Professor Skelton says boldly that it was "made public through ecclesiastical channels. " It would be interesting to know his authority for this statement. The writer of this article says it was published as the result of a calculated indiscretion by the Liberal board of strategy. As it was through his agency that publication of the letter was sought and secured, it will be agreed that he speaks with knowledge. It does not, of course, follow that Laurier was a party to its publication.

The campaign of 1896 was on both sides lively, violent and unscrupulous. The Conservatives had two sets of arguments; and so had the Liberals. Those of us who watched the campaign in Quebec at close range know that not much was said there by the Liberals about the high crime of coercing a province. Instead, stress was laid upon the futility and inadequacy of the proposed remedial legislation; upon the high probability that more could be got for the minority by negotiation; upon the suggestion that, negotiation failing, remedial legislation that would really accomplish something could still be invoked. This argument, plus the magic of Laurier's personality and Tarte's organizing genius, did the business. Futile the sniping of the curés; vain the broadsides of the bishops; empty the thunders of the church! Quebec went to the polls and voted for Laurier. Elsewhere the government just about held its own despite the burden of its remedial policy; but it was buried under the Quebec avalanche. The Liberals took office sustained by the 33 majority from the province which had once been the citadel of political Conservatism.

"Now is the winter of our discontent Made glorious summer by this sun of York; And all the clouds that lour'd upon our house In the deep bosom of the ocean buried. Now are our brows bound with victorious wreaths; Our bruised arms hung up for monuments; Our stern alarums changed to merry meetings; Our dreadful marches to delightful measures. "

PART TWO. LAURIER AND EMPIRE RELATIONSHIPS

WILFRID Laurier was Prime Minister of Canada from July 9, 1896, to October 6, 1911, fifteen years and three months, which, for the Dominion, is a record. Sir John Macdonald was Premier of the Dominion of Canada for over nineteen years, but this covered two terms separated by five years of Liberal rule.

The theory of government by party is that the two parties are complementary instruments of government; by periodic interchanges of position they keep the administration of the country efficient and progressive. The complete acceptance of this view would imply a readiness upon the part of a party growing stale to facilitate the incoming of the required alternative administration, but no such phenomenon in politics has ever been observed. Parties, in reality, are organized states within the state. They have their own dynasties and hierarchies; and their reason for existence is to clothe themselves with the powers, functions and glory of the state which they control. Their desire is for absolute and continuing control to which they come to think they have a prescriptive right; and they never leave office without a sense of outrage. There never yet was a party ejected from office which did not feel pretty much as the Stuarts did when they lost the throne of England; the incoming administration is invariably regarded by them in the light of usurpers. This was very much the case with the Conservatives after 1896; and the Liberals had the same feeling after 1911, that they had been robbed, as they deemed, of their rightful heritage. Parties are not, as their philosophers claim, servants of the state co-operating in its service; their real desire is the mastery of the state and the brooking of no opposition or rivalship. Nevertheless the people by a sure instinct compel a change in administration every now and then; but they move so slowly that a government well entrenched in office can usually outstay its welcome by one term of office. The Laurier administration covering a full period of fifteen years illustrates the operation of this political tendency. The government came in with the good wishes of the people and for nearly ten years went on from strength to strength, carrying out an extensive and well-considered domestic programme; then its strength began to wane and its vigor to relax. Its last few years were given up to a struggle against the inevitable fate that was visibly rising like a tide; and the great stroke of reciprocity which was attempted in 1911 was not nearly so much a belated attempt to give effect to a party principle as it was a desperate expedient by an ageing administration to stave off dissolution. The Laurier government died in 1911, not so much from the assaults of its enemies as from hardening of its arteries and from old age. Its hour had struck in keeping with the law of political change. Upon any reasonable survey of the circumstances it would be held that Laurier was fortunate beyond most party leaders in his premiership—in its length, in the measure of public confidence which he held over so long a period, in the affection which he inspired in his immediate following, and for the opportunities it gave him for putting his policies into operation.

Viewed in retrospect most of the domestic occurrences of the Laurier regime lose their importance as the years recede; it will owe its place in Canadian political history to one or two achievements of note. Laurier's chief claim to an enduring personal fame will rest less upon his domestic performances than upon the contribution he made towards the solution of the problem of imperial relations. The examination of his record as a party leader in the prime minister's chair can be postponed while consideration is given to the great services he rendered the cause of imperial and international Liberalism as Canada's spokesman in the series of imperial conferences held during his premiership.

Laurier, up to the moment of his accession to the Liberal leadership, had probably given little thought to the question of Canada's relationship to the empire. Blake knew something about the intricacies of the question. His Aurora speech showed that as early as 1874 he was beginning to regard critically our status of colonialism as something which could not last; and while he was minister of justice in the Mackenzie ministration he won two notable victories over the centralizing tendencies of the colonial office. But Laurier had never been brought into touch with the issue; and when, after assuming the Liberal leadership, he found it necessary to deal with it, he spoke what was probably the belief latent in most of the minds of his compatriots: acceptance of colonial status with the theoretical belief that some time, so far distant as not to be a matter of political concern, this status would give way to one of independence. "The day is coming, " he said in Montreal in 1890, "when this country will have to take its place among the nations of the earth.... I want my country's independence to be reached through the normal and regular progress of all the elements of its populations toward the realization of a common aspiration. " Looking forward to the issues about which it would be necessary for him to have policies, it is not probable that he put the question of imperial relationships very high. Certainly he had no idea that it would be in dealing with this matter that he would reveal his qualities at their highest and lay the surest foundation for his fame.

In 1890 Laurier, as we have seen, believed the Canadian future was to be that of colonialism for an indefinite period and then independence. In 1911, the year he left office, in a letter to a friend he said: "We are making for a harbor which was not the harbor I foresaw twenty-five years ago, but it is a good harbor. It will not be the end. Exactly what the course will be I cannot tell, but I think I know the general bearing and I am content. " The change in view indicated by these words is thus expounded by Professor Skelton: "The conception of Canada's status which Sir Wilfrid developed in his later years of office was that of a nation within the empire. " But between the two quoted declarations there lay twenty-one years of time, fifteen years of prime ministership and the experiences derived from attendance at four imperial conferences in succession—another record set by Laurier not likely ever to be repeated.

THE IMPERIALIST DRIVE

Laurier's imperial policies were forged in the fire. He took to London upon the occasion of each conference a fairly just appreciation of what was politically achievable and what was not, and there he was put to the test of refusing to be stampeded into practicable courses. Professor Skelton records two enlightening conversations with Laurier dealing with the difficulties in which the colonial representatives in attendance at these gatherings found themselves. Said Sir Wilfrid:

"One felt the incessant and unrelenting organization of an imperialist campaign. We were looked upon, not so much as individual men, but abstractly as colonial statesmen, to be impressed and hobbled. The Englishman is as businesslike in his politics, particularly his external politics, as in business, even if he covers his purposefulness with an air of polite indifference. Once convinced that the colonies were worth keeping, he bent to the work of drawing them closer within the orbit of London with marvelous skill and persistence. In this campaign, which no one could appreciate until he had been in the thick of it, social pressure is the subtlest and most effective force. In 1897 and 1902 it was Mr. Chamberlain's personal insistence that was strongest, but in 1907 and after, society pressure was the chief force. It is hard to stand up against the flattery of a gracious duchess. Weak men's heads are turned in an evening, and there are few who can resist long. We were dined and wined by royalty and aristocracy and plutocracy and always the talk was of empire, empire, empire. I said to Deakin in 1907 that this was one reason why we could not have a parliament or council in London; we can talk cabinet to cabinet, but cannot send Canadians or Australians as permanent residents to London, to debate and act on their own discretion. "

Still more enlightening is this observation:

"Sir Joseph Ward was given prominence in 1911 through the exigencies of imperialist politics. At each imperial conference some colonial leader was put forward by the imperialists to champion their cause. In 1897 it was obvious that they looked to me to act the bell-wether, but I fear they were disappointed. In 1902 it was Seddon; in 1907, Deakin; in 1911, Ward. He had not Deakin's ability or Seddon's force. His London friends stuffed him for his conference speeches; he came each day with a carefully typewritten speech, but when once off that, he was at sea. "

What was the intention of this "unrelenting imperialist campaign"? It took many forms, wore many disguises, but in its secret purposes it was unchangeable and unwearying. It was a conscious, determined attempt to recover what Disraeli lamented that Great Britain had thrown away. Twenty years after Disraeli had referred to the colonies as "wretched millstones hung about our neck, " he changed his mind and in 1872 he made an address as to the proper relations between the Mother Land and the colonies which is the very corner-stone of imperialistic doctrine. His declaration was in these words:

"Self-government, in my opinion, when it was conceded, ought to have been conceded as part of a great policy of imperial consolidation. It ought to have been accompanied by an imperial tariff; by securities for the people of England for the enjoyment of the unappropriated lands which belonged to the sovereign as their trustee; and by a military code which should have precisely defined the means, and the responsibilities, by which the colonies should be defended, and by which, if necessary, this country should call for aid from the colonies themselves. It ought, further, to have been accompanied by the institution of some representative council in the metropolis, which would have brought the colonies into constant and continuous relations with the home government. "

From the day Disraeli uttered these words down to this present time there has been a persistent, continuous, well-financed and resourceful movement looking towards the establishment in London of some kind of a central governing body—parliament, council, cabinet, call it what you will—which will determine the foreign policies of the British Empire and command in their support the military and naval potentialities of all the dominions and dependencies. It fell to Laurier to hold the pass against this movement; and this he did for fifteen years with patience, sagacity and imperturbable firmness against the enraged and embattled imperialists, both of England and Canada. Laurier, in the comment quoted above, said that in 1897 the imperialists had looked to him to act as the bell-wether. They had good reason to be hopeful about his usefulness to them. The imperial preference just enacted by the Canadian parliament had been hailed both in Canada and Great Britain as a great concession to imperialistic sentiment, whereas it was in reality an exceedingly astute stroke of domestic politics by which the government lowered the tariff and at the same time spiked the guns of the high protectionists. In 1897, when Laurier first went to England, the imperial movement was at its crescent, synchronous with the great welling up of sentiment and reverence called forth by the Diamond Jubilee of Queen Victoria. Strachey has a penetrating word about the strength which Queen Victoria's "final years of apotheosis" brought to the imperialistic movement:

"The imperialist temper of the nation invested her office with a new significance exactly harmonizing with her own inmost proclivities. The English policy was in the main a common-sense structure; but there was always a corner in it where common-sense could not enter. . .. Naturally it was in the crown that the mysticism of the English polity was concentrated—the crown with its venerable antiquity, its sacred associations, its imposing spectacular array. But, for nearly two centuries, common-sense had been predominant in the great building and the little, unexplored, inexplicable corner had attracted small attention. Then with the rise of imperialism there was a change. For imperialism is a faith as well as a business; as it grew the mysticism in English public life grew with it and simultaneously a new importance began to attach to the crown. The need for a symbol—a symbol of England's might, of England's worth, of England's extraordinary mystical destiny—became felt more urgently than before. The crown was the symbol and the crown rested upon the head of Victoria. "

To be translated from the humdrum life of Ottawa to a foremost place in the vast pageantry of the Diamond Jubilee, there to be showered with a wealth of tactful and complimentary personal attentions was rather too much for Laurier. The oratorical possibilities of the occasion took him into camp; and in a succession of speeches he gave it as his view that the most entrancing future for Canada was one in which she should be represented in the imperial parliament sitting in Westminster. "It would be, " he told the National Liberal club, "the proudest moment of my life if I could see a Canadian of French descent affirming the principles of freedom in the parliament of Great Britain. " This, of course, was nothing but the abandonment of the orator to the rhetorical possibilities of the situation. Under the impulse of these emotions he fell an easy victim to the conspiracy of Lord Aberdeen and Lord Strathcona (of which he later made complaint) by which the "democrat to the hilt" (as Laurier had proclaimed himself but a short time earlier when he had been given prematurely the knightly title at a public function) was transmuted into Sir Wilfrid Laurier. It was, therefore, not without apparent reason that the imperialists thought that they had captured for their own this new romantic and appealing figure from the premier British dominion. But when the imperial conference met, Mr. Chamberlain, as colonial secretary, encountered not the orator intent on captivating his audience, but the cool, cautious statesman thinking of the folks at home. When the proposition for the establishment of an imperial council was made by Mr. Chamberlain it was deftly shelved by a declaration which stated that in the view of the colonial prime ministers "the present political relations are generally satisfactory under existing conditions. " The wording is suggestive of Laurier, though it is not known that he drafted the statement. The skilful suspension of the issue without meeting it was certainly the tactics with which he met and blocked, in succeeding conferences, all attempts by the imperialists to give practical effect to their doctrine.

FIFTEEN YEARS OF SAYING "NO"

The role which Laurier had to play in the successive conferences was not one agreeable to his temperament. It gave no opening for his talent. It supplied no opportunities for the making of the kind of speeches at which he was a master. It kept him from the centre of the stage, a position which Sir Wilfrid Laurier had no objection to occupying. It obliged him to courses which, in the setting in which he found himself, must at times have seemed ungracious, and this must have been a trial to a nature so courtly and considerate. To the successive proposals that came before the conference, togged out in all the gorgeous garb of Imperialism, he was unable to offer constructive alternatives; for his political sense warned him that it was twenty years too soon to suggest propositions embodying his conception of the true relations of the British nations to one another. There was nothing to do but to block all suggestions of organic change designed to strengthen the centralizing of power and to await the development of a national spirit in Canada to the point where it would afford backing for a movement in the opposite direction. So Laurier had to look pleasant and keep on saying no. To Mr. Chamberlain's proposal in 1897 "to create a great council of the Empire, " No. To the proposal made at the same time for a Canadian money contribution to the navy, No. To these propositions and others of like tenor urged in 1902 by Mr. Chamberlain with all his persuasive masterfulness, No. No naval subsidy because it "would entail an important departure from the principle of Colonial self-government. " No special military force in the Dominion available for service overseas because it "derogated from the powers of self-government. " To the Pollock-Lyttleton suggestion of a Council of advice or a permanent "secretariat" for an "Imperial Council, " No, because it "might eventually come to be regarded as an encroachment upon the full measure of autonomous, legislative and administrative power now enjoyed by all the self-governing powers."

Sir Wilfrid's policy was not, however, wholly negative, for he was mainly responsible for the formal change in 1907 in the character of the periodical conferences. The earlier conferences were between the secretary of state and representatives of "the self-governing colonies. " They were colonial conferences in fact and in name—a fact egregiously pictured to the eye in the famous photograph of the conference of 1897, revealing Mr. Chamberlain complacently seated, with 15 colonial representatives grouped about him in standing postures. In 1907 the conference became one between governments under the formal title of imperial conference, with the prime minister the official chairman, as primus inter pares. It was the first exemplification of the new theory of equality.

The change of government in Great Britain in 1905 must have brought to Sir Wilfrid a profound sense of relief; it was no longer necessary to rest upon his armor night and day. Not that the Imperialist drive ceased but it no longer found its starting point and rallying place in the Colonial office. The centralists operated from without, looking about for someone to put forward their ideas, as in 1911 when they took possession of Sir Joseph Ward, New Zealand's vain and ambitious Prime Minister, and induced him to introduce their half-baked schemes into the Conference. He and they were suppressed by universal consent, Sir Wilfrid simply lending a hand. Sir Wilfrid's refusal at this conference to join Australia and other Dominions in a demand that they be consulted by the British government in matters of foreign policy seemed to many out of harmony with the Imperial policies which he had been pursuing. Mr. Asquith at this conference declared that Great Britain could not share foreign policy with the Dominions; and Sir Wilfrid declared that Canada did not want to share this responsibility with the British government. Seemingly Sir Wilfrid thus accepted, despite his repeated claim that Canada was a nation, a subordinate relation to Great Britain in the field of foreign relations which is the real test of nationhood. In fact, however, this was the crowning manifestation of his wariness and far-sightedness. He realized in 1911 what is only now beginning to be understood by public men who succeeded to his high office, that a method of consultation obviously defective and carrying with it in reality no suspensory or veto power, involves by indirection the adoption of that very centralizing system which it had been his purpose to block. If, Sir Wilfrid said, Dominions gave advice they must be prepared to back it with all their strength; yet "we have taken the position in Canada that we do not think we are bound to take part in every war. " He saw in 1911 as clearly as Lloyd George did in 1921 (as witness the latter's statement to the House of Commons in that year on the Irish treaty) that the policy of consultation gave the Dominions a shadowy and unreal power; but imposed upon them a responsibility, serious and inescapable. He thus felt himself obliged to discourage the procedure suggested by Premier Fisher of Australia, even though, to the superficial observer, this involved him in the contradiction of, at the same time, exalting and depreciating the status of his country.

LAURIER'S VIEW OF CANADA'S FUTURE

What conception was there in Laurier's mind as to the right future for Canada? He revealed it pretty clearly on several occasions;

notably in 1908 in a tercentenary address at Quebec in the presence of the present King, when he said: "We are reaching the day when our parliament will claim co-equal rights with the British parliament and when the only ties binding us together will be a common flag and a common crown. " He was equally explicit two years later when, addressing the Ontario club in Toronto, he said: "We are under the suzerainty of the King of England. We are his loyal subjects. We bow the knee to him. But the King of England has no more rights over us than are allowed him by our own Canadian parliament. If this is not a nation, what then is a nation? " Laurier looked forward to the complete enfranchisement of Canada as a nation under the British Crown, with a status of complete equality with Great Britain in the British family. A keen-witted member of the Imperial Conference of 1911, Sir John G. Findlay, Attorney-General for New Zealand, saw the reality behind the anomalous position which Sir Wilfrid held. "I recognized, " he says, "that Canadian nationalism is beginning to resent even the appearance—the constitutional forms—of a sub-ordination to the Mother country. " "And, " he added, revealing the clarity of his understanding, "this is not a desire for separation. " But it was not in London that the question of Imperial relationships presented its most thorny aspect. Laurier could maintain there a stand-pat, blocking attitude with no more disagreeable consequences than perhaps a little social chilliness, the symbolical "gracious duchess" showing a touch of hauteur and disappointment. It was in the reactions of the issue upon Canadian politics that Laurier met with his real difficulties. He could not, by tactics of procrastination or evasion, keep the question out of the domestic field; the era of abject, passive and unthinking colonialism was beginning to pass; and the spirit of nationalism was stirring the sluggish waters of Canadian politics. Sir Wilfrid had to face the issue and make the best of it. He handled the question with consummate adroitness and judgment; but ultimately its complexities baffled him and the Imperialists who wanted everything done for the Empire and the so-called "Nationalists" of Quebec, who wanted nothing done, joined forces against him.

THE CANADIAN IMPERIALISTS

It was the Imperialists in the old country and in Canada who gave the issue no rest; they believed, apparently with good reason, that a little urgency was all that was needed to make Canada the very forefront of the drive for the consolidation of the Empire. The English-speaking Canadians were traditionally and aggressively

British. The basic population in the English provinces was United Empire Loyalist, which absorbed and colored all later accretions from the Motherland—an immigration which in its earlier stages was also largely militarist following the reduction of the army establishment upon the conclusion of the Napoleonic wars. It was inspired with a traditional hostility to the American republic. The hereditary devotion to the British Crown, of which Victoria to the passing generations appeared to be the permanent and unchanging personification, threw into eclipse the corresponding sentiment in England. English-speaking Canadians were more British than the British; they were more loyal than the Queen. One can get an admirable idea of the state of Ontario feeling in the addresses at the various U. E. L. celebrations in the year 1884; in both its resentments and its affections there was something childish and confiding.

Imperialism, on its sentimental side, was a glorification of the British race; it was a foreshadowing of the happy time when this governing and triumphant people would give the world the blessing of the pax Britannica. "We are not yet, " said Ruskin in his inaugural address, "dissolute in temper but still have the firmness to govern and the grace to obey. " In this address he preached that if England was not to perish, "she must found colonies as fast and far as she is able, " while for the residents of these colonies "their chief virtue is to be fidelity to their country (i. e. England) and their first aim is to be to advance the power of England by land and sea. " Seely got rid of all problems of relationship and of status by expanding England to take in all the colonies; the British Empire was to become a single great state on the model of the United States. "Here, too, " he said, "is a great homogeneous people, one in blood, language, religion and laws, but dispersed over a boundless space. " Such a conception was vastly agreeable to the more aggressive and assertive among the English Canadians. It kindled their imagination; from being colonists of no account in the backwash of the world's affairs, they became integrally a part of a great Imperial world-wide movement of expansion and domination; were they not of what Chamberlain called "that proud, persistent, self-asserting and resolute stock which is infallibly destined to be the predominating force in the future history and civilization of the world"? Moreover, it gave them a sense of their special importance here in Canada where the population was not "homogeneous in blood, language and religion; " it was for them, they felt, to direct policy and to control events; to take charge and see that developments were in keeping with suggestions from headquarters overseas.

What these Canadian parties to the great Imperial drive thought of Sir Wilfrid's dilatory, evasive and blocking tactics is not a matter of surmise. Upon this point they did not practise the fine art of reticence; and their angry expostulations are to be found in the pages of Hansard, in the editorial pages of the Conservative press, in the political literature of the time, in heavy condemnatory articles which found publication through various mediums. Thus Sir George Foster could see in Laurier's statements to the Ontario club nothing but "foolish, even mischievous talk. " "If, " he added, "they are merely for the sake of rhetorical adornment they are but foolish. If, however, they are studied and serious they are revolutionary. " And to the extent that they could they made trouble for Sir Wilfrid, in which labor of love they were energetically assisted, upon occasion, by high officials from the other side of the Atlantic. Laurier had five years of more or less continuous struggle with Lord Minto, a combination of country squire and heavy dragoon, who was sent to Canada as governor-general in 1898 to forward by every means in his power the Chamberlain policies. He busied himself at once and persistently in trying to induce the Canadian government to commit itself formally to the policy of supplying Canadian troops for Imperial wars. In the spring of 1899 he wanted an assurance which would justify the war office in "reckoning officially" upon Canadian troops "in case of war with a European power; " in July he urged an offer of troops in the event of war in South Africa which "would be a proof that the component parts of the Empire are prepared to stand shoulder to shoulder to support Imperial interests. " With the outbreak of the South African war, Lord Minto regarded himself less as Governor-General than as Imperial commissioner charged with the vague and shadowy powers which go with that office; and Sir Wilfrid had, in consequence, to instruct him on more than one occasion that Canada was still a self-governing country and not a military satrapy. Professor Skelton does nothing more than barely allude to these troubles; the story, which would be most interesting and suggestive, will perhaps never be told. But some idea of what was afoot can be drawn from the fact that at a public gathering in Montreal in the month of November, 1899, Lord Minto was advised and instructed by an active politician and leading lawyer that under his powers as the representative of Imperial authority he could order the Canadian militia to South Africa without reference to the Canadian parliament!

Associated with Lord Minto in the applying of Imperial pressure to the Canadian government was General Hutton, commander of the

Canadian forces. In those days this position was always filled by an Imperial officer who was given leave of absence in order that he might fill the position. He was thus a Canadian official, paid out of the Canadian treasury and subject to the Canadian government; but few of the occupants of the office were capable of appreciating this fact. They regarded themselves as representatives of the war office with large but undefined powers in the exercise of which they frequently found themselves in conflict with the Canadian government. General Hutton's interfering activities were so objectionable that he was got rid of by a face-saving expedient; but four years later a successor to his office, Lord Dundonald, was formally dismissed by order-in-council for his "unpardonable indiscretion" in publicly criticizing the acting minister of militia. Lord Minto, unofficially advised by military officers and opposition politicians, resisted signing the order-in-council until it was made clear to him that the alternative would be a general election in which the issue would be his refusal. The incident was conclusive as to the necessity of having a Canadian at the head of the Canadian forces—a change which was subsequently effected.

These controversies and conflicts of opinion became factors in Canadian politics. The Conservatives sought in the general elections of 1900 to make an issue out of the government's hesitation in taking part in the South African war in advance of the meeting of parliament; this, plus injudicious and provocative speeches by the incalculable Mr. Tarte and the general indictment of Laurier as lukewarm towards the cause of a "united Empire" weakened the Liberals in Ontario; but this loss was easily off-set by gains elsewhere. Again in 1904 the Dundonald issue was effective only in Ontario which, in keeping with what appears to be an instinctive political process, was beginning to consolidate itself as a make-weight against the overwhelming predominance of Liberalism in Quebec. In the 1908 elections the Imperial question was almost quiescent in the English provinces; but it was beginning to emerge in a different guise and with aspects distinctly threatening to Laurier in his own province.

"COLONIALISM INGRAINED AND IMMITIGABLE"

Laurier in resisting the Chamberlain push knew that even English-Canada, long somnolent under a colonial regime, was not in the mood to accept the radical innovations that were being planned in Whitehall; and he knew, still better, that his own people would be against the programme to a man. The colonialism of the French-Canadians was immitigable and ingrained. They had secured from the British parliament in 1774 special immunities and privileges as the result of Sir Guy Carleton's hallucination that given these the French-Canadian habitant would assist the British authorities in chastising the rebellious American colonists into submission. These privileges, continued and embodied in the act of confederation, were enjoyed by the French-Canadians—as they believed—by virtue of Imperial guarantees; they held that they were safe in their enjoyment only While there was in the last analysis British control over Canada and while the final judgment on Canadian laws was passed by British courts. But their colonialism, unlike that of the English-Canadians, was of a quality that could never be transmuted into Imperialism. The racial mysticism of that movement repelled them; and still more they were deterred by the cost and dangers of Imperialistic adventure. It was for England, in return for their whole-hearted acceptance of colonial subordination, to protect them internally against any courses by the English-Canadians which they might choose to regard as an infringement of their privileged position and externally against all danger of invasion or conquest.

If Sir Wilfrid had been called upon to choose only between these two camps he could perhaps have made a choice which would not have been ultimately a political liability. But the situation was not so simple. There was a third factor which, alike by inclination and political necessity, Sir Wilfrid had to take into account. This was Canadian nationalism, in contrast with the racial nationalism of which Mr. Bourassa was the apostle. The backing upon which Sir Wilfrid relied at first to resist the military and naval policies of the Imperialists was the timidity and reluctances of colonialism; but he knew that this was at best a temporary expedient. To urgings that Canada should assist in the upkeep of the Imperial navy by money contributions and should also maintain special militia forces available for service in Imperial wars overseas, Sir Wilfrid felt that some more plausible reply than a brusque refusal was necessary; and he met them with the contention that Canada must create military and naval forces for her own defence which would be available for the wars of the Empire at the discretion of the Canadian parliament. These views put forward almost tentatively in 1902 ultimately bore fruit in definite policies of national defence. Thus the answer to demand for naval contribution, to which policy all the other Dominions had subscribed, was to declare that Canada should have her own navy; and this took form, after numerous skirmishes with admiralty opinion, which was scandalized at the suggestion, in the Naval Service Bill of 1910.

This course, which was thus urged upon Sir Wilfrid by events, earned him the displeasure of both the Imperialists and the Little Canadians. To the former Laurier's policy seemed little short of treasonable, particularly his insistence that while Canada was at war when England was at war the extent, if any, of Canada's participation in such war must be determined solely by the Canadian parliament. His own countrymen on the other hand viewed with disquietude these first halting steps along the road of national preparedness; might it not lead by easy gradations to that "vortex of militarism" against which Sir Wilfrid had voiced an eloquent warning? Where there is opinion capable of being exploited against a government the exploiter soon appears. In Quebec, Monk, Conservative, and the Nationalist, Bourassa, who entering Parliament as a follower of Laurier had developed a strong antipathy to him, were indefatigable in alarming the habitant by interpreting to him the secret purposes of the naval service bill. It was nothing, they claimed, but an Imperialistic device by which the Canadian youth would be dragged from his peaceful fireside to become cannon fodder in the Empire's wars. Meanwhile in the English provinces, the government's policy was fiercely attacked as inadequate and verging upon disloyalty by the Imperialists. The Conservative opposition, after one virtuous interlude in 1909 when they showed a fleeting desire to take a non-political and national view of this matter of defence, could not resist the temptation to profit by the campaign against the government's policy; and they joined shrilly in the derisive cry of "tin pot navy. " These onslaughts from opposite camps were a factor in the elections of 1911; especially in Quebec where twenty-seven constituencies (against eleven in 1908) elected opponents of Laurier.

POLICIES THAT ENDURE

Sir Wilfrid fell; but his Imperial policies lived. During the campaign the old country Imperialists had been very busy from Rudyard Kipling down—or up—in lending aid to the forces fighting the Liberal government; and its defeat was the occasion for much rejoicing among them. Mr. A. Bonar Law, M. P., doubtless voiced their views when he predicted under the incoming regime, "a real advance towards the organic union of the Empire. " All these hopes, like many which preceded them, were short-lived; for Sir Robert

Borden, once he got his bearings, took over the Laurier policies and widened them. In that significant fact the clue to these policies is found. They were not personal to Laurier, owing their coolness towards perfervid Chamberlainism to his lack of English blood as his critics held; they were in fact national policies dictated by the necessities of the times. To the casual student of the development of Imperial relations for the decade following 1896, it might seem that the Liberal conception of an Empire evolving steadily into a league of free nations was only saved from destruction by the fortunate circumstance that Sir Wilfrid Laurier was during those years the representative of Canada at successive Imperial conferences; but this would be, perhaps, to put his services too high. Canada's public men have never failed her in the critical times in her history when attempts were made through ignorance or design to turn her aside from the high road to national sovereignty; as witness Gait in 1859, Blake in his long duel with Lord Carnarvon, Sir John A. Macdonald in 1885, when he resisted the premature demand for a Canadian contingent for service in the Soudan, Tupper in the early nineties when his vigorous resistance to the proposal that Canada should pay tribute for protection had something to do with the demise of the Imperial Federation League. Any man fit to be premier of Canada would have taken pretty much the position that Sir Wilfrid did. This does not in the least detract from the credit due Laurier. The task was his and he discharged it with tact, ability, patience and courage. For his services in holding their future open for them every British Dominion owes the memory of Laurier a statue in its parliament square.

PART THREE. FIFTEEN YEARS OF PREMIERSHIP

There have been prime ministers of Canada casually thrown up by the tide of events and as casually re-engulfed; but Wilfrid Laurier was not one of them. There may have been something accidental in his rise to leadership, but his capture of the premiership was a solid political achievement. The victory of June 23, 1896, crowned with triumph the daring strategy of the campaign. But popular opinion regarded the victory as a gift of the gods. The wheel of fortune spinning from the hands of fate had thrown into the high office of the premiership one about whose qualifications there was doubt even in the secret minds of many of his supporters. He was a man of charming manners and of gracious personality. His carriage on the platform and the grace and finish of his speaking had fascinated the public imagination. But what likelihood was there that these qualities would enable him to deal adequately with the harsh realities, the stubborn problems which he must face as premier? Most unlikely, it was generally agreed. The Conservatives, though profoundly chagrined at the trick fate had played upon them, looked forward with pleasurable expectation to the revenge that would be theirs when Laurier, political dilettante and amateur, took up the burden that had been too great for their own Ulysses. They foresaw a Laurier regime which for futility and brevity would take its place in history with the ill-starred prime ministership of Mackenzie. The average Liberal felt that the government, which would get its driving force and executive power from someone else—identity not yet revealed—would have in Laurier a most attractive and genial figurehead. These illusions long persisted, though there was little excuse for them on election night and still less a month later when the Laurier cabinet was in being.

To be a Rouge and to be in Montreal during the three weeks following the glorious 23rd of June was the height of felicity. After nearly 50 years of proscription and impotence in their own province, they were triumphant and dominant. Moreover, since they had supplied the majority which made possible the taking of office by the Liberals, they would be triumphant and dominant as well in the Dominion field. Among the election occurrences which they regarded as specially providential was the defeat of Tarte in Beauharnois. If he had been elected it might have been necessary for Laurier to do something for him, but now that he had fallen upon the glacis of the impregnable fortress he had elected to assail, who were they to repine over the doings of fate? "The Moor has done his work; the Moor can go! " Moreover, had he not been for long an inveterate Bleu? Had he not actually been the organizer of Bleu victory when Laurier experienced his memorable defeat in Drummond-Arthabaska in 1877? His defeat made it possible to have a simon-pure Rouge contingent from Quebec.

While they were thus indulging in roseate day-dreams the actual business of cabinetmaking was going forward, with Tarte at Laurier's right hand as chief adviser from Quebec. The writer has a very clear recollection of a long conversation which he had at that time with Tarte. Much of it was given up to picturesque and forthright denunciation by Tarte of the means by which he had been defeated in Beauharnois. The mill-owners at Valleyfield, he said, had lined up their operatives and had given them the option of voting for Bergeron or getting out. The worth to a country of an industrial system which makes political serfs of its workmen was vigorously challenged in language which had little resemblance to the harangues which led to Tarte's undoing six years later. From this he went on to speak of Laurier's qualities and the amazing ignorance of them shown even by his intimates of his own race. There had been much speculation in Montreal as to who should be the new high commissioner for Canada in London. Sir Donald A. Smith, who had been appointed in the last weeks of Conservative rule, would be, it was assumed, dismissed. Tarte scouted the idea that Smith would be disturbed. Laurier was not that kind of a man. He would not dismiss Smith; he would make friends with him. Sir Donald was a man of affairs, and so was Laurier; they would co-operate with one another. "These people do not understand Laurier; he has a governing mind; he wants to do things; he has plans; he will walk the great way of life with anyone of good intention who will join him. " With much more to the same effect. To Tarte, who was his intimate, Laurier at this moment did not appear as one overcome with his destiny and drifting with the tide, but as the resolute captain of the ship, who knew where he wanted to go, had a fairly clear idea as to how to get there, and also knew whom he wanted with him on the voyage. Later on Tarte forgot about this.

THE MAKING OF THE GOVERNMENT

There was verification of Tarte's estimate in the job of cabinet-making turned out by Laurier in July. In building the government the lines of least resistance were not followed. A dozen men who deemed themselves sure of cabinet rank found themselves overlooked; five of fifteen portfolios went to men imported from provincial arenas without Dominion parliamentary experience. Laurier knew the kind of government he wanted and he provided himself with such a government by the direct method of getting the colleagues he desired wherever he could find them. No doubt he found plenty of employment for his sunny ways in placating his disappointed colleagues. In time there were consolation prizes for all, for this one a judgeship, for that one a lieutenant-governorship, for the next a life seat in the senate; the phalanx of fighting second-raters who had done valuable work in opposition, reinforcing and buttressing the work of the front benches disappeared gradually from parliament. And with those he chose he too had his way, as witness the side-tracking of Sir Richard Cartwright to the dignified but at the time relatively unimportant department of trade and commerce. Between Sir Richard and the Canadian manufacturers there was a blood feud. It was not Sir Wilfrid's intention to make the feud his own or even to agree to it being carried on by Sir Richard. He took for minister of finance, W. S. Fielding, who justified his choice by successfully steering the budget bark between Scylla and Charybdis for fourteen years in succession before the whirlpool finally sucked him down. Where Laurier went outside his following for colleagues he had equally definite ends to serve.

The care with which Laurier chose his colleagues, and his indifference to personal appeal, should have been proof sufficient to the public that he was a prime minister who looked forward and planned for the future. And the plan? Why to stay in power for the longest possible period of time. It is as natural for a government to want to stay in power as it is for a man to want to live; nor is there in this anything discreditable. A prime minister is sure that he desires to retain power in order that he may serve the country as no rival could conceivably serve it; and even if the desire fades and is replaced by a lively appreciation of the personal satisfactions which can be served by the office, no real prime minister notices the transformation. The ego and the country soon become interblended in his mind. A prime minister under the party system as we have had it in Canada is of necessity an egotist and autocrat. If he comes to office without these characteristics his environment equips him with them as surely as a diet of royal jelly transforms a worker into a queen bee.

Laurier saw that an efficient government, harmonious in its policies and ably led, would afford a contrast to the preceding administration that must forcibly impress the Canadian people. He, therefore created a government of all the talents. Anxious for discreet handling of the difficult fiscal problem he turned to Nova Scotia for W. S. Fielding. Foreseeing the possibility of grave constitutional problems arising he put the portfolio of justice into the hands of the wisest and most venerable of Liberals, Sir Oliver Mowat. Recognizing that a backward and stagnant west meant failure for his administration he placed the department of interior, which had become a veritable circumlocution office, under the direction of the ablest and most aggressive of western Liberal public men, Clifford Sifton. The time was to come when other values were to hold in relation to cabinet appointments; but in the beginning efficiency was the test, at least in intention. It was thus Laurier proposed in part to build foundations under his house that it might endure. And to insure that virtue should not lack its reward he proceeded to buttress the edifice by a second line of support.

In the general election of 1896 the Liberal strategy had been to give the party managers in the English provinces an apparent choice of the best weapons, but with all these advantages the results showed that they had barely held their own. The majority came from Quebec where Laurier had apparently to face the heaviest odds. The natural inference was not lost upon Laurier. If he was to remain in power he must look to Quebec for his majority. A majority was necessary and he must get it where it was to be had. This decision was at first probably purely political. The consequences were not fully foreseen, that to get this support a price would have to be paid—by the Liberals of the other provinces. Still less was it foreseen that the overwhelming support of his own people would become not only politically essential to Laurier but a moral necessity as well— something which in time he felt, by an imperious demand of the spirit, that he must hold even though this allegiance became not a political asset but a liability. Gradually, perhaps insensibly at first, in opposition possibly to his judgment, certainly to his public professions oft repeated, he came to regard it as necessary to so shape party policy as always to command the approval of French-Canadian public opinion. Sir Wilfrid lived to see, as the culmination of 20 years of this policy, the French and the English-Canadians more sharply divided than they had been for 80 years. Such is the capacity of the human mind for self-deception that he could see in this divergence nothing but the proof that his life's work had been destroyed by envious and designing men.

THE FOUNDATION STONE OF POLICY

Quebec in turning Laurierite did not turn Liberal. This was the factor hidden from the public eye that governed the future. The Laurier sweep of Quebec in 1896 was the result of a combination of the Bleu and Rouge elements. The old dominant French-Canadian party had been made up of Bleus and Castors—factions bitterly divided by differences of temperament, of outlook and belief, and still more by desperate personal feuds between the leaders. When the coming of responsible government broke up the solidarity of the French-Canadians they separated into three groups, the controlling factor in each case being religious belief. The Castors were ultra-clerical and ultramontane; the Bleus inherited the tradition of Gallicanism; the Rouges imported and adapted the anti-clericalism of European Liberals. Various influences—the brilliance and resourcefulness of Cartier's leadership and antipathy to Rouge extremism among them—kept Bleu and Castor in an uneasy alliance. This alliance began to disintegrate when Laurier rose to the command of the Liberals. There was a steady drift from the Bleu to the Liberal camp—by this time the old definition of "Rouge" was under taboo; and in 1896 the Bleus moved over almost in a body. This was not an altogether instinctive and voluntary movement; it was suggested, inspired, successfully shepherded and safely delivered.

Tarte's confidence that Laurier could win Quebec was not based wholly upon faith in the power of Laurier's personal appeal. He was himself a Bleu leader brought into accidental relations with the Liberals. His breach with the Conservatives began as one of the unending Castor-Bleu feuds. His knowledge of the McGreevy-Connolly frauds gave him the power, as he thought, to blow the Castor chief, Sir Hector Langevin—a cold, selfish, greedy, domineering, rather stupid man—into thinnest air, thus opening the road to the leadership of the French-Conservatives to his friend and leader, the brilliant, unscrupulous and ambitious Chapleau. He over-estimated his power. The whole strength of the government at Ottawa was at once concentrated in keeping the lid on that smouldering cauldron of stench and rottenness, the system of practical politics of that day. The Conservative chiefs tried to suppress Tarte and he refused to be suppressed—there was not a drop of coward's blood in his veins. Then they set to work to destroy him. He sought a refuge and he found it—in parliament, to which he was elected in 1891 as an Independent as the result of an arrangement with Laurier. As he used to say, it was a case of parliament or jail for him.

Inevitably, in following up his charges in parliament, Tarte was thrown into more and more intimate relations with the Liberal leaders. He knew that for him there was no Conservative forgiveness; as he was wont to say: "I have spoiled the soup for too many. " It was not long before Sir John Thompson could congratulate Laurier, in one of the sharpest sayings parliament ever heard, upon having among his lieutenants—"the black Tarte and the yellow Martin. " For ten years he remained Laurier's chief lieutenant in Quebec, but he never in any sense of the word became a Liberal, though in 1902, just before he was thrown from the battlements, he busied himself in reading lifelong Liberals out of the party. Chapleau, who was Tarte's confidant and ally, though he was also a member of the Dominion government, became Lieutenant-governor of Quebec and retired to Spencer Wood, but not to forget politics among its shades. When the peculiar developments of the Dominion campaign of 1896 made it evident that Conservative victory in Quebec under the virtual leadership of the bishops meant the permanent domination of the Castors, the whole Bleu influence was thrown to the Liberals.

Professor Skelton's life of Laurier does not take us much behind the scenes. It is in the main a record of political events, with comments upon Laurier's relations to them. Laurier's letters, mostly to unnamed correspondents, are of slight interest, but to this there are a few notable exceptions. There are letters between Laurier, Tarte and Chapleau of the greatest political value. They make clear to a demonstration, what shrewd political observers of that day surmised, that there was a definite political understanding between these three men. This explains the composition of the Quebec delegation in the Laurier government. Apart from Laurier there was in it no representative of French Catholic Liberalism, unless the purely nominal honor of minister without portfolio given to C. A. Geoffrion is to be taken as giving this representation. C. A. did not put the honor very high. "I am, " he said, "the mat before the door. " Tarte, a Quebecker and a Bleu, became Montreal's representative at Ottawa. Disappointment among the Liberals led first to rage and then to rage plus fear as Tarte with the magic wand of the patronage and power of the public works department, began to make over the party organization in the province. Open rebellion under François Langelier broke out in December: "A coalition with Chapleau, " Langelier informed the public, "is under way. " But the rebellion died away. The Laurier influence was too strong. Langelier was quite right in his statement. The coalition movement at that time was far advanced. The letter from Chapleau to Laurier, bearing date February 21, 1897, quoted by Professor Skelton, was that of one political intimate to another. Take this paragraph as an illustration: "The Castors in the battle of June 23rd lost their head and their tail; their teeth and claws are worn down; even breath is failing for their cries and their movements and I hope that before the date of the Queen's jubilee we shall be able to say that this race of rodents is extinct and figures only in catalogues of extinct species. " The reference to the coming extinction of the Castors had relation to the then pending provincial elections as to which he made certain references to political strokes which "I am preparing. " Associated with this Laurier-Tarte-Chapleau triumvirate was a fourth, C. A. Dansereau, nominally postmaster of Montreal, actually the most restless political intriguer in the province of Quebec. Dansereau had been the brains of the old Senecal-Chapleau combination which had dominated Quebec in the eighties. Just what Laurier thought of the company he was now keeping was a matter of record for he had set it forth in a famous article in L'Electeur in 1882 entitled "The Den of Thieves, " which led to L. A. Senecal, the Bleu "boss, " prosecuting him for criminal libel. Laurier stood his trial in Montreal, pleaded justification, and after a hard fought battle won a virtual triumph through a disagreement of the jury with ten of the jurymen favorable to acquittal.

LAST ROUND WITH THE BISHOPS

Little wonder that Francois Langelier, his brother Charles, and other associates of Laurier in the lean years of proscription were consumed with indignation that Laurier should pass them by to associate with his former enemies. They did not realize the political necessity that controlled Laurier's course. Laurier had great need to hold his new allies for his position in Quebec for the first year or so of office was precarious. The Manitoba school question had still to be settled. Laurier was political realist enough to know that he would have to take what he could get and this he would have to dress up and present to the public as his own child. He knew that the bishops, chagrined, humiliated, enraged by their election experience, were only waiting for the announcement of settlement to open war on him. It would then depend upon whether or not they were more successful than in June in commanding the support of their people. In Laurier's own words: "They will not pardon us for their check of last summer; they want revenge at all costs. "

The real fight, it was recognized, would be in Rome. Thither there went within two months of the Liberals taking office, two emissaries of the French Liberals, the parish priest of St. Lin, a lifelong, personal and political friend of Laurier, and Chevalier Drolet, one of the Canadian papal Zouaves, who had rallied to the defence of the Holy City twenty-six years before. There followed swiftly two more distinguished intermediaries, Charles Fitzpatrick, solicitor-general of Canada, and Charles Russell, of London, son of Lord Russell of Killowen. Backing them up was a petition to the pope signed by Laurier and forty-four members of parliament, protesting against the political actions of the Canadian episcopate. Nor did the Canadian hierarchy lack representation in Rome. While this conflict of influence was in progress at Rome, the terms of the Manitoba school settlement were made public in November, 1896. The settlement embodied substantial concessions in fact, but Archbishop Langevin and his fellow clerics at once fell upon it. Langevin denounced it as a farce. To Cardinal Begin it appeared an "indefensible abandonment of the best established, most sacred rights of the Catholic minority. " A regime of religious proscription was inaugurated. Public men were subjected to intimidation; Liberal newspapers were banned, among them L'Electeur, the chief organ of the party. The bishops destroyed themselves by their violence. Rome does not lightly quarrel with governments and prime ministers. By March Mgr. Merry Del Val was in Canada as apostolic delegate; and though care was taken to save the faces of the bishops, their concerted assaults upon the government ceased. Laurier had never again to face the embattled bishops, which is not the same thing as saying that they ceased to take a hand in politics. As Professor Skelton truly remarks: "The Archbishop of Montreal, Monseigneur Paul Bruchesi, who kept in close touch with Wilfrid Laurier, soon proved that sunny ways and personal pressure would go further than the storms and thunderbolts of the doughty old warrior of Three Rivers. " With the bishops silenced, Laurier's foes in Quebec found the issue valueless to them. Their political associates from other provinces, after the disappointment of 1896, would not consent to a revival of the question. One of the party leaders declared he would not touch it with a forty-foot pole. Tupper formally erased it from the party calendar. The question remained quiescent; but Laurier always remained in fear of its re-emergence; and with cause. The resentments it left went underground and later had a revival in the passionate zeal with which the Quebec clergy embraced the faith of nationalism as preached by Bourassa. In one respect the school question and its settlement proved useful. It was the exhibit unfailingly displayed to prove upon needed occasions that the charge was quite untrue that in directing party policy Laurier was unduly sensitive to Quebec sentiment. In effect it was said: "Laurier made Quebec swallow in 1896; now it is your turn"—a formula which finally became tedious through repetition.

SUPREME IN QUEBEC

The second issue which appeared for a moment to put Laurier's grip on Quebec in peril was the South African war. Looking back twenty-three years it is pretty clear that Laurier's position at the outbreak of the war, that the Canadian parliament should be consulted as to the sending of a contingent, was wholly reasonable. Those were the days of heady Imperialism in the English provinces; and, vigorously stirred up by Laurier's party foes for political purposes, it struck out with a violence which threatened to bring serious political consequences in its train. Tarte was credited with having declared publicly in the Russell House rotunda: "Not a man nor a cent for South Africa, " which did not help matters. The storm was so instant and threatening that Laurier and his colleagues bowed before it. By order-in-council Canada authorized the sending of a contingent. Other contingents followed, and Canada took part in the war on terms of limited liability which were agreeable to both the British and Canadian governments.

The South African war was most unpopular with the French-Canadians, but the unpopularity did not extend to Laurier. They agreed in theory with Bourassa but they recognized that Laurier had yielded to force majeure. Indeed the very violence with which Laurier was assailed in Ontario strengthened his hold in Quebec. It is not easy for a proud people to stomach insults such as, for instance, the remark in the Toronto News, that the English-Canadians would find some way of "emancipating themselves from the dominance of an inferior people whom peculiar circumstances had placed in authority in the Dominion. " The election of 1900 gave Laurier fifty-eight supporters in the province of Quebec out of a total of sixty-five seats. The Rouge-Bleu coalition had not come off officially, Chapleau's death in 1898 having removed the necessity of formally recognizing his services, but the coalition of Bleu and Rouge elements had taken place; and it held so firmly that when some of the architects of the fusion tried later to undo their work they found this could not be done. Dansereau was the first to go. Mr. Mulock, the postmaster-general, entirely oblivious of the fact that Dansereau was one of the main wheels in the Quebec machine and seeing in him only an entirely incapable postmaster, fired him in 1899 with as little hesitation as a section boss would show in bouncing an incompetent navvy. Tarte and Laurier tried to patch up the quarrel, but Dansereau preferred to return to journalism as editor of an independent journal whose traditions were Conservative. He was to be, five years later, one of the leaders in that curious conspiracy, the MacKenzie-Mann-Berthiaume-La Presse deal—the details of which as told by Professor Skelton read like a detective yarn—which was turned into opera bouffe by Laurier's decisive and timely interference. In 1902, Tarte, in Laurier's absence and in the belief that he could not resume the premiership on account of illness, attempted to seize the successorship by pre-emption, and was promptly dismissed from office by Laurier. Tarte and Dansereau tried to rally the Bleu forces against Laurier, but these were no longer distinguishable from the Liberal hosts into which they had merged. Their day was over and their power gone. Laurier reigned supreme.

These commitments and considerations furnished the background to the drama of Laurier's premiership. Much that took place on the fore-stage is only intelligible by taking a long vision of the whole setting. There was nothing of assertiveness or truculence in this steady movement by which Liberal policy and outlook was given a new orientation, Quebec replacing Ontario as the determinant. Students of politics can trace the changing influence through the fifteen years of Liberal rule, in legislation, in appointments and in administrative policies. One or two illustrations might be noted.

A CHALLENGE AND A CHECK

During the crisis of 1905 over the school provisions in the Autonomy bills erecting Alberta and Saskatchewan into provinces, Walter Scott, M.P., in a letter quoted by Professor Skelton, refers to the "almost unpardonable bungling" which had brought the crisis about. But Sir Wilfrid did not step into this difficulty by mischance. He knew precisely what he was doing though he did not foresee the consequences of his action because with all his experience and sagacity he never could foretell how political developments would react upon the English-Canadian mind. The educational provisions of the autonomy bill were designed to remove the still lingering resentment of Quebec over the settlement of the Manitoba school question and to further this purpose Sir Wilfrid indulged in his speech introducing these bills in that entirely gratuitous laudation of separate schools which had on Ontario and western Canadian opinion the enlivening effect of a match thrown into a powder barrel. This incident revealed not only the tendency of Laurier's policy but illustrated the tactics which he had developed for achieving his ends in the face of opposition within the party. Upon occasions of this kind he was addicted to confronting his associates and followers with an accomplished fact, leaving no alternative to submission but a palace rebellion which he felt confident no one would attempt. By such methods he had already rounded several dangerous corners, as for instance his committing Canada to submit her case in the matter of the Alaska boundaries to a tribunal without an umpire—though it was the clearly understood policy of the Canadian government and the Canadian parliament to insist upon an umpire; and he resorted again to a stroke of this character in 1905. Professor Skelton's story of the crisis is the official version, but there is another version which happens to be more authentic.

Following the general election of 1904, the government decided to deal without further delay with the matter of setting up the new provinces. It was known that there was danger of revival of the school question, for during the election campaign a Toronto newspaper had sought to make this an issue, contending that the delay in giving the provinces constitutions was due to the demand of the Roman Catholic church that they should include a provision for separate schools. The policy agreed upon by the government was to continue in the provincial constitutions the precise rights enjoyed by the minority under the territorial school ordinances of 1901. There was a vigorous controversy in parliament as to whether the autonomy bills in their original form kept faith with this understanding. Sir Wilfrid Laurier and Mr. Fitzpatrick, minister of justice, contended vehemently that they did. Clifford Sifton, who was the western representative in the cabinet and the party most directly interested, held that they did not. Mr. Sifton was absent in the Southern States when the bill was drafted. He reached Ottawa on his return the day after Sir Wilfrid had introduced the bills to parliament. He at once resigned. Fielding, who had also been absent, was credited with sharing to a considerable extent Sifton's view that the bill introduced did not embody the policy agreed upon. The resulting crisis put the government in jeopardy. A considerable number of members associated themselves with Mr. Sifton and the government was advised that their support for the measure could only be secured if clauses were substituted for the provisions in the act to which objection was taken. To make sure that there would be no mistake that the substituted provisions should merely continue the territorial law as it stood, they insisted upon drafting the alternative clauses themselves. Sir Wilfrid, acutely conscious that this constituted a challenge to his prestige and authority, used every artifice and expedient at his command to induce the insurgents either to accept the original clause or alternatives drafted by Mr. Fitzpatrick; for the first time the tactical suggestion that resignation would follow noncompliance was put forward. The dissentient members stood to their guns; Sir Wilfrid yielded and the measure thus amended commanded the vote of the entire party with one Ontario dissentient.

The storm blew over but the wreckage remained. The episode did Laurier harm in the English provinces. It predisposed the public mind to suspicion and thus made possible the ne temere and Eucharist congress agitations which were later factors in solidifying Ontario against him. In Quebec it gave Mr. Bourassa, whose hostility to Laurier was beginning to take an active form, an opportunity to represent Laurier as the betrayer of French Catholic interests and to put himself forward as their true champion. "Our friend, Bourassa, " wrote Sir Wilfrid to a friend in April, 1905, "has begun in Quebec a campaign that may well cause us trouble. " From this moment the Nationalist movement grew apace until six years later it looked as though Bourassa was destined to displace Laurier as the accepted leader of the French Canadians. It was only the developments of the war that restored Laurier to his position of unchallenged supremacy.

In Manitoba also there were evidences of Sir Wilfrid's preoccupation with the business of never getting himself out of touch with Quebec public opinion. For years he sought by private and semi-public negotiations to get the Winnipeg school board to come to a modus vivendi with the church by which Catholic children would be segregated in their own schools within the orbit of the public school system, but failed, partly owing to the non possumus attitude of Archbishop Langevin, who was not prepared to be deprived of a grievance which enabled him to mix in Quebec and Manitoba politics. The Liberal policy of accepting provincial electoral lists for Dominion purposes resulted in the Manitoba lists being compiled under conditions to which the Liberals of this province strongly objected, and they fought for years to secure a right to final revision under Dominion auspices. Twice they pressed their case with such vigor that the government undertook to pass the requested legislation but on both occasions resistance in the house by the Conservatives led to the prompt withdrawal of the measure by Sir Wilfrid. In both cases Manitoba Liberals knew quite well that the difficulty was not the opposition of the Conservatives but the opposition of Laurier. They were advised that Laurier was apprehensive of the effect of the proposed legislation upon public opinion in Quebec. He feared the criticism by his opponents that while Laurier would not interfere with Manitoba when it was a matter of the educational rights of the minority he was willing to interfere when it was a matter of obliging his political friends. There was something too in the charge that the delay in dealing with the matter of the extension of the Manitoba boundaries arose from the same feeling. To transfer the Northwest territories, where the minority had certain constitutional rights in matters of education, to Manitoba where the minority had none would be to put one more weapon into the hands of Mr. Bourassa. The extension of Manitoba's boundaries had to await a change in administration.

THE TALE OF FIFTEEN YEARS.

There is always a temptation to the biographer of a prime minister to relate his hero to the events of his period as first cause and controlling spirit—the god of the storm; whereas prime ministers, like individuals, are the sports of destiny; things happen and they have to make the best of them. The performances of the Laurier government may be divided into two classes, those due to its own initiative and those which were imposed by circumstances. The ratio between the two classes changed steadily as the administration grew in age. After the impetus born of the reforming zeal of opposition and the natural and creditable desire to fulfil express engagements dies away, the inclination of a government is not to invite trouble by looking around for difficult tasks to do. "Those who govern, having much business on their hands, " says Benjamin Franklin, "do not like to take the trouble to consider and carry into execution new projects. " This is a political law to which all governments conform. Even the great reforming administration of Gladstone which took office in 1868, had earned five years later the famous jest of Disraeli: "The ministers remind me of one of those marine landscapes not very unusual off the coast of South America; you behold a range of extinct volcanoes; not a flame flickers upon a single pallid crest. "

Fifteen years of Liberal rule in Canada furnish a complete field for the study of the party system under our system. In 1896 a party stale in spirit, corrupt and inefficient, went out of office and was replaced by a government which had been bred to virtue by eighteen years of political penury. It entered upon its tasks with vigor, ability and enthusiasm. It had its policies well defined and it set briskly about carrying them out. A deft, shrewd modification of the tariff helped to loosen the stream of commerce which after years of constriction began again to flow freely. There was a courageous and considered increase in expenditures for productive objects. A constructive, vigorously executed immigration policy brought an ever expanding volume of suitable settlers to Western Canada which in turn fed the springs of national prosperity. This impulse lasted through the first parliamentary term and largely through the second, though by then disruptive tendencies were appearing. By its third term the government was mainly an office-holding administration on the defensive against an opposition of growing effectiveness. And then in the fourth term there was an attempt at a rally before the crash. The treatment of the tariff question, always a governing factor in Canadian politics even when apparently not in play, is an illustration of the government's progress towards stagnation. The 1897 tariff revision "could not, " says Professor Skelton, "have been bettered as a first preliminary step toward free trade. " "Unfortunately, " he adds, "it proved to be the last step save for the 1911 attempt to secure reciprocity. " After 1897 Laurier's policy was to discourage the revival of the tariff question. Tarte's offence was partly that he did not realize that sleeping dogs should be allowed to lie. "It is not good politics to try to force the hand of the government, " wrote Laurier to Tarte. And he added: "The question of the tariff is in good shape if no one seeks to force the issue. " With Tarte's ejection there followed nearly eight years during which real tariff discussion was taboo. Then under the pressure of the rising western resentment against the tariff burdens, the government turned to reciprocity as a means by which they could placate the farmers without disturbing or alarming the manufacturers. By what seemed extraordinary good luck the United States president, Republican in politics, was by reason of domestic political developments, in favor of a reciprocal trade agreement. It seemed as though the Laurier government as by a miracle would renew its youth and vigor; but the situation, temporarily favorable, was so fumbled that it ended not in triumph but in defeat.

The disasters of the Laurier railway policy—or rather lack of policy—must always weigh heavily against the undoubted achievements of the Laurier regime. A period of marked national expansion gave rise to all manner of railway ambitions and schemes, and Laurier lacked the practical capacity, foresight and determination to fit them into a general, well-thought-out, practicable scheme of development. Again it was a case of letting the pressure of events determine policy, in place of policy controlling events. He could not deny the Grand Trunk's ambitions, but he obliged it to submit to modifications demanded by political pressure which turned its project, perhaps practicable in its original form, into a huge, ill-thought-out transcontinental enterprise. Equally he could not hold the ambitions of Mann and McKenzie in check. The advisability of a merger of these rival railway groups was obvious at the time, but Laurier let them each have their head, dividing government assistance between them, with resulting ruin to both and bequeathing to his successors a problem for which no solution has yet been found.

PERSONAL GOVERNMENT

During the years of his premiership Laurier rose steadily in personal power and in prestige. It is in keeping with the genius of our party system that the leader who begins as the chosen chief of his associates proceeds by stages, if he has the necessary qualities, to a position of dominance; the republic is transformed into an absolute monarchy. In the government of 1896 Laurier was only primus inter pares; his associates were in the main contemporary with him in point of years and public service. Their places had been won by party recognition of their services and abilities. In the government of 1911 Laurier was the veteran commander of a company which he had himself recruited. Of his 1896 colleagues but few remained, and of these only Mr. Fielding had kept his relative rank in the party hierarchy. All his remaining colleagues had entered public life long subsequent to his accession the Liberal leadership. Not one had been in parliament prior to 1896. Their entrance into public life, their steps in promotion, their admittance to the government were all subject to his approval, where they were not actually due to his will. To Laurier's authority they yielded unquestioning obedience, and with it went a deep affection inspired and made sure by the personal consideration and kindliness that marked his relations with them. Under these conditions, men of strong, individual views and ambitions, with reforming temperaments and a desire to force issues, did not find the road to the Privy Council open to them; different qualities held the password.

In 1908 Sir Wilfrid, when a discerning electorate had deprived him of a colleague whose political incapacity had been completely demonstrated, became a party to a deal by which he re-entered parliament. An old friend took the liberty of asking Sir Wilfrid why he wanted this associate back in the cabinet, only to be told that "So-and-So never made any trouble for me. " At least twice in the last four years of his regime Sir Wilfrid, conscious of the waning energies of his party, took advice outside of his immediate circle as to what should be done; on both occasions he rejected advice tendered to him because this involved the inclusion in the cabinet of personalities that might have disturbed the charmed serenity of that circle. Sir Wilfrid preferred to have things as they were, perhaps because his sense of reality warned him that, so far as the duration of time during which he would hold office was concerned, there probably would not be any great difference between a government wholly agreeable to him and one reconstituted to meet the demand of the younger and more vigorous elements in the party. In 1909, in a letter to a supporter who had lost the party nomination for his constituency, he gave premonition of his own fate: "What has happened to you in your county will happen to me before long in Canada. Let us submit with good grace to the inevitable. "

The inevitable end in the ordinary course of events would have been the going on of the party until it died of dry rot and decay, as the Liberals had already died in Ontario; but fortunately, both for the party and for Laurier's subsequent fame—though it may not have seemed so at the time—emergence of the reciprocity question gave it an opportunity to fall on an issue which seemed to link up the end of the regime with its heroic beginnings and to reinvest the party with some of its lost glamor.

LAURIER: DEFEAT AND ANTI-CLIMAX

THE defeat of the Liberals in September, 1911, raised sharply the question of the party's future and the leadership under which it would face that future. Speaking at St. Jerome toward the close of the campaign Sir Wilfrid had stated positively that if defeated he would retire. This declaration of intention—no doubt at the moment sincerely made—was designed to check the falling away from Laurier's leadership in Quebec, which was becoming more noticeable as election day drew near. But the appeal was ineffective.. The effective opposition to Laurier in Quebec came not from Borden or from Monk, the official leader of the French Conservatives, but from Bourassa. Laurier and his lieutenants fought desperately, but in vain, to break the strengthening hold of the younger man on the sympathies of the French electors. In Quebec the custom of the joint open air political meeting is still popular, and at such a concourse in St. Hyacinthe, an old Liberal stronghold, Sir Wilfrid's colleagues, Lemieux and Beland, met a notable defeat at the hands of Bourassa— an incident which clearly revealed how the winds were blowing. Bourassa, fanatically "nationalist" in his convictions and free from any political necessity to consider the reactions elsewhere of his doctrines, was outbidding Sir Wilfrid in the latter's own field. Laurier received the news of the electoral result in a hall in Quebec East, surrounded by the electors of the constituency which had been faithful to him for 40 years. He accepted the blow with the tranquil fortitude which was his most notable personal characteristic; but the feature in the disaster which must have made the greatest demand upon his stoicism was this indication that his old surbordinate and one time friend was—apparently—about to supplant him in the leadership of his own people. The election figures showed that whereas Laurier had carried 49 seats in Quebec in 1896, 58 in 1900, 54 in 1904 and again in 1908, he had been successful in only 38 constituencies against 27 for the Conservatives and Nationalists combined. Laurier, at the moment of his defeat, was within two months of entering upon his 70th year. He had been 40 years in public life; for 24 years leader of his party; for 15 years prime minister. He had had a long and distinguished career; and he had gone out of office upon an issue which, with confidence, he counted upon time to vindicate. He had long cherished a purpose to write a history of his times. The moment was, therefore, opportune for retirement; and it must be assumed that he gave some thought to the advisability or otherwise of living up to his St. Jerome pledge. But neither his own inclination nor the desire of his followers pointed to retirement; and the next session of parliament found him in the seat he had occupied twenty years before as leader of the opposition. The party demand for his continuance in the leadership was virtually unanimous. There was only one possible successor to Sir Wilfrid— Mr. Fielding. But he was not in parliament. Also he was in disfavour as the general whose defensive plan of campaign had ended in disaster. His name suggested "Reciprocity"—a word the Liberals were quite willing, for the time being, to forget. He was left to lie where he had fallen. For some years he lived in political obscurity, and it was only the emergence of the Unionist movement which made possible his re-entrance to public life and his later career.

THE REVIVAL OF LIBERAL HOPES

When Sir Wilfrid resumed the leadership after the formality of tendering his resignation to the party caucus it meant, in fact, that he intended to die in the saddle. Thereafter Sir Wilfrid talked much about the inexpediency of continuing in the leadership, and often used language foreshadowing his resignation—indeed the letters quoted by Professor Skelton in the latter chapters of his book abound in these intimations—but these came to be regarded by those in the know as portents: implying an intention to insist upon policies to which objections were likely to develop within the party.

Notwithstanding the severity of their defeat—they were in a minority of 45 in the House—the Liberals in opposition showed a good fighting front, and ere long hope revived. The Borden government found itself in difficulties from the moment of taking office—largely by reason of the tactics by which Laurier's supremacy in Quebec had been undermined. The Nationalist chiefs declined an invitation to enter the government, but they controlled the Quebec appointments to the cabinet, and thus assumed a quasi-responsibility for the new government's policy. The result was disastrous to them; for the Borden government, subject to the influences that had enabled it to sweep Ontario, could not concern itself with the preservation of Bourassa's fortunes. The extension of the Manitoba boundaries was a blow to the Nationalists; they failed in their efforts to preserve the educational rights of the minority in the added territory. Laurier had evaded this issue; Borden could not evade it, and by its settlement Bourassa was damaged. Still more disastrous to the Nationalist cause was the naval policy which Mr. Borden submitted to Parliament in the session of 1912-1913. There was in its presentation an ingenious attempt to reconcile the irreconcilable which deceived nobody. The contribution of the three largest dreadnoughts that could be built was to satisfy the Conservatives; the Nationalists were expected to be placated by the assurance that this contribution was merely to meet an emergency, leaving over for later consideration the question of a permanent naval policy. But all the circumstances attending the setting out of the policy—the report of the admiralty, the letters of Mr. Churchill, the speeches by which it was supported with their insistence upon the need for common naval and foreign policies—made it only too clear that it marked the abandonment of the Canadian naval policy which had been entered upon only four years before with the consent of all parties and the acceptance in principle of the Round Table view of the Imperial problem. Laurier challenged the proposition whole-heartedly. Here was familiar fighting ground. From the moment they joined battle with the government the Liberals found their strength growing. They were indubitably on firm ground. They were helped mightily by Mr. Churchill's attempted intervention in which he belittled Canadian capacity in a manner worthy of Downing street in its palmiest days. Mr. Churchill had the bright idea of coming to Canada to take a hand personally in the controversy. A Canadian-born member of the British House of Commons sounded out various Canadians as to the nature of the reception Mr. Churchill would receive. Mr. Churchill did not come— fortunately for the government. The Liberals fought the proposition so furiously in the Commons that the government had to introduce closure to secure its passage through the commons, whereupon the Liberal majority in the Senate threw it out. The Liberal policy was to challenge the government to submit the issue to the people in a general election. That within eighteen months from the date of their disastrous defeat the Liberals should invite a second trial of strength spoke of rapidly reviving confidence. The government ignored the challenge, for very good reasons. In the sequel Laurier, as with all his policies having to deal with Imperial questions, was amply justified. The policy of Dominion navies was never again seriously questioned in Canada; when admiralty officials, true to form, challenged it in 1918 it was Sir Robert Borden who defended it, to some purpose.

These developments were fatal to Quebec Nationalism as a distinct political force under the direction of Mr. Bourassa. The ideas that inspired it did not lapse. Nor did Mr. Bourassa, as apostle of these ideas, lose his personal eminence. But the electors in sympathy with these ideals began to develop views of their own as to the political action required by the times. Their alliance with the Conservatives had brought them no satisfaction. They had ejected the most eminent living French-Canadian from the premiership to the very evident injury of Quebec's influence in Confederation—that about represented the sum of their achievements. The thought that they had been on the wrong track began to grow in their minds. The conditions making for the creation of the Quebec bloc were developing. The disposition was to get together under a common leadership. It was still a question as to whether, in the long run, that leader should be Laurier or Bourassa; but all the conditions favored Laurier. For one thing, he could command a large body of support outside of his own province which it was quite beyond the power of Bourassa to duplicate. The swing to Laurier was so marked that by 1914 the confident prediction was made by good political judges that if there were an election Laurier would carry 60 out of the 65 seats in Quebec. Such a vote meant victory. Sir Wilfrid was slow in coming to believe that an early reversal of the decision of 1911 was possible; but finally found himself infected with the hopefulness of his following. Hard times became a powerful ally of the Liberals and the government suffered from the first shock of the impending railway collapse. The course of the party lay clear before it; it was to see that the conditions in Quebec remained favorable and to await, with patience, the coming of an election which would reopen the doors to office. But not too much patience, for the years were slipping past. Laurier was in his 73rd year.

THE PARTIES AND THE WAR

Such were the political conditions: a government in a position of growing doubtfulness and a combative and confident opposition— when Canada found herself plunged over night into the Great War. Under the high emotion of this venture into the unknown politics vanished for a brief moment from the land. If that moment could have been seized for a sacred union of hearts dedicated to the great task of carrying on the war how different would the whole future of Canada have been! In the fires of war our sectional and racial intractibilities might have been fused into an enduring alliance. But Canadian statesmanship was not equal to the opportunity. For this Sir Wilfrid has no accountability. There is no question of the correctness and generosity of his attitude as revealed in the war session of August, 1914. From a speech in the next session it might be inferred that he would have gone farther than he did if overtures had been made to him.

In Canada, as elsewhere, the war spelt opportunity for more than the patriot and the hero. The schemer, resolute to make the war serve his ends, appeared everywhere. From the morrow of those first days of high exaltation the two currents ran side by side in Canada: the clear tide of valor and self-sacrifice, the muddy stream of cowardice and self-seeking. There was an influential element in the dominant party which was determined to exploit the war to the limit for political and personal interests. The war meant patronage; it must be placed where it would do the most party good. It meant an opportunity for artificial and perfectly safe distinction; this must be employed for increasing the political availability of friends. Political colonels began to adorn the landscape. It meant a corking good issue upon which an election could be won; why not take advantage of it? While the government officially was leading a united people into action, these scheming political profiteers were perfecting their plans for appealing to the people on the ground that the government—a party government which had not invited any measure of close co-operation from the opposition—must have a mandate to carry on the war. There is a quite authentic story of a leading Canadian being cheered up on a train journey by assurances from a travelling companion, a friend holding high office, that events were shaping for certain victory; until he learned that the enemy about to be defeated was the "damn Grits. " The battle of Ypres in April, 1915, saved Canada from an ignoble general election on the meanest of issues. Though some of the conspirators still pressed for an election, it soon became apparent that the proposal was abhorrent to public opinion. Canadians could not bring themselves to the point of fighting one another while their sons and brothers were dying side by side in the mud of Flanders.

The danger of a profound division of the Canadian people in war-time passed; but irretrievable damage had been done to the cause of national unity. In considering subsequent events these unhappy developments of the first year of the war cannot be overlooked. Party feeling among the Liberals had been held in leash with difficulty; now it was running free again. The attitude of the party towards the government was in effect: "You have tried to play politics with the war; very well, you will find that this is a game that two can play at. " The strategy looking to a future trial of strength was skilfully planned. There was no challenge to the government plans. It was given full liberty of action upon the understanding that it would accept full responsibility and be prepared to render an account in due time to parliament and people. The tactics were those of paying out the rope as the government called for it. The attitude of the Liberal leaders towards the war was unexceptionable. Sir Wilfrid's recruiting speeches—and he made many of them—were admirable; and he did not hesitate to point the way of duty to the young men of his own province. Upon things done or not done the attitude of the parliamentary Liberals was increasingly critical; and the government, it must be said, with its scandals over supplies, its favoritism in recruiting, its beloved Ross rifle, gave plenty of opportunity to opposition critics. With every month that passed the political advantage that had come to the government, because it was charged with the task of making war, waned.

General elections were due in the autumn of 1916. It became a serious question of Liberal policy to decide between agreeing to an extension of the life of parliament, which the government intended to request, and the forcing of an election. Two lieutenants of Sir Wilfrid toured Western Canada sounding Liberal opinion; their disappointment was obvious when, in a conference with a group of Liberals in Winnipeg, they found opinion solidly adverse to an election. Their reasons for an election were plainly stated—in brief they were that on the details of its war management the government could be, and, in their judgement, should be, beaten. But Sir Wilfrid, with his hand on the country's pulse, could not be stampeded. He saw, more clearly than his lieutenants, the danger to the party of refusing an extension at that time. A twelve months was added to the life of parliament with a reservation in the minds of the Liberals that the first extension would be the last. This meant an election in 1917.

THE NATIONALISTS AND ONTARIO

Mr. Bourassa was acutely conscious of the development of opinion in Quebec favorable to the Liberals, and he sought to retain his hold upon his following by the tactics which in the first place had given him his following—by going to extremes and outbidding Laurier. The chief article in the Nationalist creed was that Canada was everywhere a bilingual country, French being on an equality with English in all the provinces. This contention rested upon a conglomeration of arguments, assertions, assumptions, inferences, and it was backed by thinly disguised threats of political action. The opposing contention that bilingualism had a legal basis only in Quebec and in the Dominion parliament with its services and courts was interpreted as an insult. Mr. Lavergne, the chief lieutenant of Mr. Bourassa, was wont to wax furiously indignant over the suggestion, as he put it, that he must "stay on the reservation" if he was to enjoy the privileges that he held to be equally his in whatever part of Canada he might find himself.

Events in Ontario put the test of reality to the Nationalist theories. A feud broke out between the English-speaking and the French-speaking Catholics over the language used for instruction in separate schools where both languages were represented; and resulting investigation revealed a state of affairs suggesting something very like a conspiracy to minimize or even abolish the use of English in all school areas where the French were in control. Resulting regulations and legislation intended to put a stop to these conditions gave French a definitely subordinate status. This fired the heather, and later somewhat similar action by Manitoba added fuel to the flames. The Nationalist agitation was resumed with increased vehemence in Quebec; and the Ontario minority were encouraged to defy the regulations by assurances that means would be found to bring Ontario to time. In addition to legal action (which brought in the end a finding by the Privy Council completely destroying the Nationalist claim that bilingualism was implied in the scheme of Confederation) various ingenious attempts were made to apply pressure to Ontario. The most daring, and in results the most disastrous, was the threat that if Ontario did not remove the "grievances of the minority" the people of Quebec would go on strike against further participation in the war. That dangerous doctrine operating upon a popular mind impregnated with suspicion of the motives and intentions behind Canada's war activities, produced the situation which made inevitable the developments of 1917. The movement against Ontario was Nationalist in its spirit, its inspiration and its direction. Side by side with it went a Nationalist agitation of ever-increasing boldness against the war. Ammunition for this campaign was readily found in the imputations, innuendoes, charges, mendacities of the Labor and pacifist extremists of Great Britain and France; they lost none of their malignancy in the retelling. Bourassa included Laurier in the scope of his denunciations. Laurier's loyal support of the war and his candid admonitions to the young men of his own race made him the target for Bourassa's shafts. Something more than a difference of view was reflected in Bourassa's harangues; there was in them a distillation of venom, indicating deep personal feeling. "Laurier, " he once declared in a public meeting, "is the most nefarious man in the whole of Canada. " Bourassa hated Laurier. Laurier had too magnanimous a mind to cherish hate; but he feared Bourassa with a fear which in the end became an obsession. He feared him because, if he only retained his position in Quebec, Liberal victory in the coming Dominion elections would not be possible. Laurier feared him still more because if Bourassa increased his hold upon the people, which was the obvious purpose of the raging, tearing

Nationalist propaganda, he would be displaced from his proud position as the first and greatest of French-Canadians. Far more than a temporary term of power was at stake. It was a struggle for a niche in the temple of fame. It was a battle not only for the affection of the living generation, but for place in the historic memories of the race. Laurier, putting aside the weight of 75 years and donning his armor for his last fight, had two definite purposes: to win back, if he could, the prime ministership of Canada; but in any event to establish his position forever as the unquestioned, unchallenged leader of his own people. In this campaign—which covered the two years from the moment he consented to one year's extension of the life of parliament until election day in 1917—he had repeatedly to make a choice between his two purposes; and he invariably preferred the second. In the sequel he missed the premiership; but he very definitely accomplished his second desire. He died the unquestioned leader, the idol of his people; and it may well be that as the centuries pass he will become the legendary embodiment of the race—like King Arthur of the English awaiting in the Isle of Avalon the summons of posterity. As for Bourassa, he may live in Canadian history as Douglas lives in the history of the United States—by reason of his relations with the man he fought.

THE BILINGUAL EPISODE

The Canadian house of commons was the vantage point from which Sir Wilfrid carried on the operations by which he unhorsed Bourassa. Here we find the explanation of much that appears inexplicable in the political events of 1916 and 1917. Laurier was out to demonstrate that he was the true champion of Quebec's views and interests, because he could rally to her cause the support of a great national party. Hence the remarkable projection of the bilingual issue into the proceeding of parliament in May, 1916. The question as an Ontario one could only be dealt with by the Ontario authorities once it was admitted—Sir Wilfrid being in agreement—that disallowance was not possible. Yet Sir Wilfrid brought the issue into the Dominion parliament. If he had done this merely for the purpose of making his own attitude of sympathy with his compatriots in Ontario clear, the course would have been of doubtful political wisdom, in view of his responsibilities to the party he led. But he insisted upon a formal resolution being submitted. Professor Skelton, in the passages dealing with this episode, shows him whipping up a reluctant party and compelling it, by every influence he could command, to follow him. The writer, arriving in Ottawa when this situation was developing, was informed by a leading Liberal member of parliament that the "old man" had thought out a wonderful stroke of tactics by which he was going to strengthen himself in Quebec and at the same time do no harm in Ontario—a feat beside which squaring the circle would be child's play. Very brief enquiry revealed the situation. Sir Wilfrid was determined to have a resolution and a vote. The western Liberals were in revolt; the Ontario Liberals were reluctant but were prepared to be coerced; most of the maritime province Liberals were obedient, but there was a minority strongly opposed. Theoretically the formula that there was to be no coercion, each member voting as his conscience directed, was honored; but Sir Wilfrid had found it necessary to indicate that if in the outcome it should be found that any considerable number of his supporters were not in agreement with him, he would be obliged to interpret this as indicating that the party no longer had confidence in him. Professor Skelton supplies the evidence that Sir Wilfrid pressed the threat to resign almost to the breaking point. He actually wrote out something which was supposed to be a resignation before the Ontario Liberals capitulated. The western Liberals were of sterner stuff; they stood to their guns. No resignation followed. "The defection of the western Liberals, " says Professor Skelton, "forced from Sir Wilfrid a rare outbreak of anger. " The use of the word "defection" is enlightening, as showing Professor Skelton's attitude towards the Liberals who in those trying times adhered to their convictions against the party whip. He is a thorough-going partisan, which, in an official biographer, is perhaps the right thing.

The writer's activities in encouraging opposition to these party tactics led to a long interview with Sir Wilfrid, in which there was considerable frank language used on both sides. Sir Wilfrid gave every indication that he was profoundly moved by what he called "the plight of the French-Canadians of Ontario. " They were, he said, politically powerless and leaderless; the provincial Liberal leaders, who should have been their champions, had abandoned them; the obligation rested upon him to come to their rescue. The suggestion that, while he might be within his rights in thus expressing his individual views, he should not seek to make it a party matter in view of the strong differences of opinion within the party, was rather impatiently brushed aside. Still less respect was shown the observation that it was not desirable that the Liberal party should identify itself with a resolution the carrying of which meant a general election in the height of the war upon a race and religious issue. Sir Wilfrid, in the course of the conversation, touched quite frankly upon the necessities of the Quebec political situation. He advanced the argument, which was put forward so persistently a year later, that it must be made possible for him to keep control of Quebec province, since the only alternative was the triumph of Bourassa extremism, which might involve the whole Dominion in conflict and ruin.

The episode passed apparently without disruptive results; but surface indications were misleading. In reality a heavy blow had been struck at the unity of the Liberal party; there began to be questionings in unexpected quarters of the Laurier leadership. What had happened was only too clear, to those who looked at the situation steadily. Party policy had been shaped with a single eye to Quebec necessities; and party feeling, party discipline, the personal authority of Laurier has been drawn on heavily to secure acceptance of this policy by Liberals who did not favor it. But there is in politics, as in economics, a law of diminishing returns. A year later the same tactics applied to a situation of greater gravity ended in disaster. The split which came in 1917 followed pretty exactly the split that would have come in 1916 over bilingualism, had the Liberal members not been constrained by their devotion to party regularity to vote against their convictions.

THE MOVEMENT FOR NATIONAL GOVERNMENT

The movement for national government long antedated the emergence of the issue of conscription; it was, in its origin, Liberal. Its most persistent advocates in the later months of 1916 and the opening months of 1917 were Liberal newspapers, among them the Manitoba Free Press; and there was an answer from the public which showed that the appeal for a union of all Canadians who were concerned with "getting on with the war" made a deep appeal to popular feeling. The most determined resistance came from the Conservatives. The ministerial press could see nothing in it but a Grit scheme to break up the Borden government, which they lauded as being in itself a "national government" of incomparable merit. But that movement was equally disconcerting to the Liberal strategists since it threatened to interfere with their plans for a battle, to end, as they confidently believed, in a Liberal victory. In January, 1917, Sir Wilfrid could see nothing in the movement but an attempt to prevent a French-Canadian from succeeding to the premiership, and wrote in those terms to N. W. Rowell.

An offer by Sir Robert Borden to Sir Wilfrid Laurier to join him in a national government would have been unwelcome at any time excepting perhaps in the first months in the war; but in the form in which it finally came, in May, 1918, it was trebly unacceptable. Sir Wilfrid was asked to help in the formation of a national government to put into effect a policy of conscription, already determined upon. Although history will no doubt confirm the bona fides of Sir Robert's offer, it cannot but be lenient to Sir Wilfrid's interpretation of it as a political stroke intended to disrupt the Liberal party and rob him of the premiership. From his viewpoint it must have had exactly that appearance. Laurier's position in Quebec had been undermined in the years preceding the war by the Nationalist charge that his naval and military policies implied unlimited participation, by means of conscription, in future Imperial wars. He had always denied this; and when Canada entered the great war he, to keep his record clear, was careful to declare over and over again that Canadian participation by the people collectively, and by the individual, was and would remain voluntary. As the strain of the war increased the feeling in Quebec in its favor, never very strong, grew less. There began to be echoes of Bourassa's open anti-war crusade in the Liberal party and press. Sir Wilfrid, watching with alert patience the development of Quebec opinion, began cautiously to replace his earlier whole-hearted recognition of the supreme need of defeating Germany at all costs by a cooler survey of the situation in which considerations of prudent national self-interest were deftly suggested. The "We-have-done-enough" view was beginning to prevail; and Laurier, intent upon the complete capture of Quebec at the impending elections, while he did not subscribe to it, found it discreet to hint that it might be desirable to begin to think about the wisdom of not too greatly depleting our reserves of national labor. To Laurier, thus engaged in formulating a cautious war policy against the day of voting, came the invitation from Borden to join him in a movement to keep the armies of Canada in the field up to strength by the enforcement of conscription. Every aspect of the proposition was objectionable to Laurier. It meant handing back to Bourassa the legions he had won from him, and with them many of his own followers. No one was justified in believing that Laurier with all his prestige and power could commend conscription to more than a minority of his compatriots. Sir Robert Borden's proposal meant the foregoing of the anticipated party victory at the polls, the renouncement of the premiership, and the loss, certainly for the immediate future and probably for all time, of the affection and regard of his own people as a body. The proposition doubtless looked to him weird and impossible, and not a little impudent. The argument that the proposed government could better serve the general interests of the public, or even the cause of the war, than a purely Liberal government, of which he would be the head, probably struck him as presumptuous. Three days before Sir Robert Borden made his announcement of an intention to introduce conscription, Sir Wilfrid, anticipating the announcement, wrote to Sir Allan Aylesworth his unalterable opposition to the policy. This being the case, there never was a chance that Laurier would entertain Borden's offer to join him in a national government.

THE LIBERAL DISRUPTION

Sir Wilfrid, rejecting Borden's offer, adhered to his plan of an election on party lines; but he knew that conditions had been powerfully affected by these developments. His position in Quebec was now secure and unchallenged—even Bourassa, recognizing the logic of the situation, commended Laurier's leadership to his followers. If he could hold his following in the English provinces substantially intact the result was beyond question. He set himself resolutely to the task. Thereafter the situation developed with all the inevitableness of a Greek tragedy to the final catastrophe. Sir Wilfrid surveyed the field with the wisdom and experience of the veteran commander, and from the disposition of his forces and the lay of the land he foresaw victory. But he overlooked the imponderables. Forces were abroad which he did not understand and which, when he met them, he could not control. He counted upon the strength of party feeling, upon his extraordinary position of moral authority in the party, upon his personal hold upon thousands of influential Liberals in every section of Canada, upon the lure of a victory which seemed inevitable, upon the widespread and justified resentment among the Liberals against the government for things done and undone to keep the party intact through the ardors of an election. One thing he would not do; he would not deviate by an inch from the course he had marked out. Repeated and unavailing efforts were made to find some formula by which a disruption of the party might be avoided. One such proposition was that the life of the parliament should be extended. This would enable the government, with its majority and the support it would get from conscriptionist Liberals, to carry out its programme accepting full responsibility therefor. Sir Wilfrid rejected this; an election there must be. This was probably the only expedient which held any prospects of avoiding party disruption; but after its rejection Liberals in disagreement with

Laurier still sought for an accommodation. There was a continuous conference going on for weeks in which all manner of suggestions were made. They all broke down before Laurier's courteous but unyielding firmness. There was the suggestion that the Liberals should accept the second reading of the Military Service Act and then on the third reading demand a referendum; rejected on the ground that this would imply a conditional acceptance of the principle of compulsion. There was the proposal that Laurier should engage, if returned to power, to resort to conscription if voluntary recruiting did not reach a stipulated level—not acceptable. Scores of men had the experience of the writer; going into Laurier's room on the third floor of the improvised parliamentary offices in the National History Museum, spending an hour or so in fruitless discussion and coming out with the feeling that there was no choice between unquestioning acceptance of Laurier's policy or breaking away from allegiance to him. Not that Laurier ever proposed this choice to his visitors. He had a theory—which not even he with all his lucidity could make intelligible—that a man could support both him and conscription at the same time. There is an attempt at defining this policy in a curious letter to Wm. Martin, then premier of Saskatchewan, which is quoted by Skelton. Sir Wilfrid in these conversations—as in his letters of that period, many of which appear in Skelton's Life—never failed to stress conditions in Quebec as compelling the course which he followed; the alternative was to throw Quebec to the extremists, with a resulting division that might be fatal. There was, too, the mournful and repeated assertion—which abounds also in his letters—that these developments showed that it was a mistake for a member of the minority to be the leader of the party. At the close of the session, when it became increasingly evident that a party split was impending, there were reports that Laurier proposed to make way for a successor upon some basis which might make an accommodation between the two wings of the party possible; and there was an attempt by a small group of Liberal M. P.'s to bring this about. The treatment of this incident in Professor Skelton's volume is obscure. In any case it had no significance and it came to nothing. Laurier alike by choice and necessity retained the leadership.

Sir Wilfrid misjudged, all through the piece, the temper and purpose of the Liberals who dissented from his policy. For his own courses and actions there was a political reason; he looked for the political reasons behind the actions of those in disagreement with him. He found what he looked for, not in the actual facts of the situation but in his imagination. He saw conversion to the Round Table view of the Imperial problem and the acceptance of dictation from London — a very wild shot this! He saw political ambition. He saw unworthy desires to forward personal and business ends. But he did not see what was plain to view — that the whole movement was derived from an intense conviction on the part of growing numbers of Liberals that united national action was necessary if Canada was to make the maximum contribution to the war. There was very little feeling against Sir Wilfrid — rather a sympathetic understanding of the position in which he found himself; but they were wholly out of agreement with his view that Canada was in the war on a limited liability basis. In the very height of the controversy Sir Wilfrid could not be got to go beyond saying that Canada should make enquiries as to how many men she could afford to spare from her industries and these she should send if they could be induced voluntarily to enlist. This was wholly unsatisfactory to those who held that Canada was a principal in the war, and must shrink from no sacrifices to make victory possible. Still less satisfactory was the professed attitude of the Liberal candidates in Quebec; with few exceptions they embraced the anti-war Nationalist programme. It became only too evident that a Liberal victory would mean a government dependent upon and controlled by a Quebec bloc pretty thoroughly committed to the view that Canada had "done enough. " For those committed to the prosecution of the war to the limit, conscription became a test and a symbol; and ultimately the pressure forced reluctant politicians to come together in the Union government. There followed the general election and the Unionist sweep. Laurier returned to parliament with a following of eighty-two in a house of 235. Of these 62 came from Quebec; and nine from the Maritime provinces. From the whole vast expanse from the Ottawa river to the Pacific Ocean ten lone Liberals were elected; of these only two represented the west, that part of Canada where Liberal ideas grow most naturally and freely. The policy of shaping national programmes to meet sectional predilections, relying upon party discipline and the cultivation of personal loyalties to serve as substitutes elsewhere had run its full course — and this was the harvest!

THE LAST YEAR

The events of 1917 were both an end and a beginning in Canada's political development. They brought to a definite close what might be called the era of the Great Parties. Viscount Bryce, in a work based

Laurier: A Study in Canadian Politics

upon pre-war observations, in dealing with Canadian political conditions, said:

"Party (in Canada) seems to exist for its own sake. In Canada ideas are not needed to make parties, for these can live by heredity, and, like the Guelfs and Ghibellines of mediaeval Italy, by memories of past combats; attachment to leaders of such striking gifts and long careers as were Sir John Macdonald and Sir Wilfrid Laurier, created a personal loyalty which exposed a man to reproach as a deserter when he voted against his party. "

For these conditions there were reasons in our history. Our parties once expressed deep divergencies of view upon issues of vital import; and each had experienced an individual leadership that had called forth and had stereotyped feelings of unbounded personal devotion. The chiefships of Laurier and Macdonald overlapped by only four years, but they were of the same political generation and they adhered to the same tradition. The resemblances in their careers, often commented upon, arose from a common attitude towards the business of political management. They conceived their parties as states within the state. Perhaps it would be more accurate to say they conceived them as co-ordinate with the state. Of these principalities they were the chieftains, chosen in the first place by election—as kings often were in the old times; but thereafter holding their positions by virtue of personal right and having the power in the last analysis by their own acts to determine party policy and to enforce discipline. Their personalities made these assumptions of power appear not only inevitable, but proper. Personal charm, human qualities of sympathy and understanding; an inflexible will which, except in crises, worked by indirection; the prestige of office and the glamor of victory; and the accretions of power which came from the passage of time—half their followers towards the end of their careers could not remember when other suns shone in the firmament; all these influences helped to transform party feeling into that blind worship which drew from Viscount Bryce his mordant comment.

This venerable but archaic political system did not survive the war. Beside the loyalties inspired by the war tribal devotion to a party chief seemed a trivial concern. Canadians, who gave first place to the need of getting on with the war, viewed with consternation the readiness of elements in both parties to put their political interests above the safety and honor of the commonwealth. The movement for national political unity was born of their concern and indignation.

This development was almost as displeasing to the Conservative partisans as to the Liberal "legitimists, " who upheld the right, under all circumstances, of Laurier to regain the premiership; and it was their inveterate and unthinking opposition that had much to do with the ultimate disruption of the union. They did not realize, until they got into the elections of 1921, that their party had disintegrated under the stresses of war.

A study of the origin, achievements, failures, downfall and consequences of Union government might be of interest, but it does not come into a survey of the life of Laurier. These matters are related to the influences that are now making over Canadian politics; they concern the leaders of to-day, all minor figures in the 1917 drama. Because the Union government passed without leaving behind it tangible and visible manifestations of its power, there are those who regard it as a mere futility—a sword-cut in the water, as the French say. But of the Union movement it might well be said: Si monumentum requiris circumspice. The spirit behind the movement passed with the war, but it left the old traditional party system in ruins. The readjustments that are going on to-day, the efforts at the realignment of parties, the attempt to newly appraise political values, and to redefine political relationships—all these things are testimony to the dissolving, penetrating power of the impulses of 1917.

But the task of attempting political reconstruction in a new world was not imposed upon Laurier. The signing of the armistice was the signal for the release of new forces; it was a great turning point in the world's history. But for Laurier the tale of his years was told. There was something fitting in the departure of the veteran with the turning of the tide. He had been a mere survival on the scene following the elections of 1917 which put into the hands of the Union government a mandate to "carry on" for the remainder of the war— which at that time gave promise of stretching out interminably. That election set bounds to his ambitions, wrote finis to his political career. "Unarm; the long day's work is o'er. " He continued to hold his rank in a party which waited upon events, knowing that the task of rebuilding and reconstruction must fall to younger hands. The serenity of mind which had sustained him in all the changes of a long and varied life did not desert him; and he looked forward with fortitude to the end now approaching. He had come a long way from the humble beginnings in St. Lin, 77 years before. Childhood; happy, carefree boyhood; a youth of gallant comradeship with the young swordsmen of a fighting political army; the ardors of a career in the making full of delights of battle with his peers; the call to the command; the conquest of the premiership; the long, crowded, brilliant years of office with their deep anxieties, crushing responsibilities, great satisfactions, substantial achievements; the bitterness of unexpected defeat; the gallant fight to win back to power ending by a stroke of fate in disaster; the final disruption of his party and the loss of old friends who had followed him in victory or defeat; these recollections must have been much in his mind during this year of afterglow. The end was fitting in its swiftness and dignity. No lingering, painful illness, but a swift stroke and a happy release. "Nothing is here for tears; nothing to wail. "

The End

Lightning Source UK Ltd.
Milton Keynes UK
UKHW011248130520
363213UK00002B/427